for the Good game family!

As you reach the experience

that will help your children

flourish,

All the best,

Judy

LIVE WIRES

WIRES

NEURO-PARENTING *to* IGNITE *your* TEEN'S BRAIN

To the grand founders of our family
—Mom's and Pop's alike—
who remain with us in spirit, a whispered thanks.
It is still a beautiful world.

To my amazing children and precious grandchildren—
strive for a life of excellence, not a life of ease;
many confuse the two.
Find peace. Find happiness in each other.

To my husband, my partner in parenting, thank you
for believing in me even before I believed in myself.

NEURO-PARENTING

Parenting strategies based on

neuroscience research which confirms that

the brain wires what it experiences—

for good or bad.

 **bright sky press**
HOUSTON, TEXAS

2365 Rice Blvd., Suite 202
Houston, Texas 77005

Library of Congress Cataloging-in-Publication Data on file with publisher.

ISBN 978-1-939055-03-3

10   9   8   7   6   5   4   3   2   1

Editorial Direction, Lucy Herring Chambers
Creative Direction, Ellen Peeples Cregan
Design, Marla Garcia

Printed in Canada through Friesens

LIVE WIRES

NEURO-PARENTING *to* IGNITE *your* TEEN'S BRAIN

**Insulating Your Child Against
COLLEGE FRENZY,
ACHIEVEMENT MANIA
& MEDIA EXPLOSION**

JUDITH WIDENER MUIR

with an Introduction by

GERARD T. BERRY, M.D.
Professor of Pediatrics, Harvard Medical School

bright sky press
HOUSTON, TEXAS

TABLE OF CONTENTS

INTRODUCTION

The still to be explored and veritable last frontier is the human brain/mind. It is the "stuff" that makes us special. No where else in our human bodies do the combinations of genetics and environment, programmed gene expression and development, plasticity and epigenetics work their magic to produce a life which expresses consciousness, cognition, language and feelings.

With her foray into the world of neuroscience, brain circuitry and epigenetics, as it applies to the developing adolescent, Judith (Judy) Widener Muir has produced a remarkable work, a blueprint on how the parent or educator should view the pliable but resilient mind of the teenager. She reviews these concepts in a clear and concise manner making it easy for the non-scientist to grasp the essence of her message and instructions.

She invites parents and educators to take a glimpse of the "new" field of epigenetics and see what its implications are for our teenagers. We are all born with chromosomal DNA inherited from our parents and conferring traits as well as the propensities for health and disease. Epigenetics informs us that gene expression—or the signals that "hard-wired" heritable elements emit—can be modified by environmental factors. While this pliability is especially pertinent in prenatal life, many neuroscientists believe that man is capable of altering or modifying gene expression in the brain even as an adult. In other words, one can, through learning and repetition, alter one's brain circuitry. This genetic quality could in fact be the molecular basis for the rehabilitation of the stroke victim. Implications abound for the impact of the teenager's environment on his or her health, education, and welfare.

Folk wisdom and common sense tell us that early childhood training could increase a child's ability to maximize his or her potential, but science now provides more windows onto why. Discoveries raise new questions, and information does not always have a direct route to becoming general knowledge and affecting practice. Interested parents, educators, doctors and scientists often struggle to incorporate new information into their specific fields because partner groups may not be as familiar with new information or may not be aware of its potential impact.

With her unique perspective as a mother, grandmother, educator and graduate of Harvard University's interdisciplinary Mind, Brain and Education program, Muir has processed and distilled information on epigenetics, neuroscience, parenting and college admissions in a way that gives it particular relevance for the parents of teenagers. Amalgamating psycho-social issues with family-child health issues, she blends and translates two areas of study that have not always seen eye-to-eye in the past. How can parents and educators create environments that allow the brain's plasticity to produce optimal genetic flourish? The information that Muir brings together in *Live Wires* represents years of broad research and focused experience. In accessible terminology, she opens the way for parents to create a home life that helps their child to learn, for educators to schedule classes and develop activities in a way that can make lasting impact on a child's passion for learning and success in school, and even for physicians to make new connections about the role of environment in a child's development.

Brain plasticity may allow us to adapt at different points in our lives. We can improve the wellbeing of the next generation when we learn how the functioning of biochemical systems can be supported to help a child become a better person and have a better life. When Muir looks at the ramifications of this information from her point of view as an Independent Educational Consultant, she compels us to take a hard look at our personal values and how we transmit them to our children. The college admission process, in particular, is notably stressful on teenagers and parents. Inadvertently, and with the best intentions, parents can make it more difficult—and in fact can hinder their child's ability to get into the best possible college—because unexamined values and a lack of understanding of scientific principles can lead them to create negative environments for their children.

Even in the best of times, college admission is a field filled with land mines. Inhabited by several groups—teens, parents, teachers, counselors, administrators and college admission officers—mystery surrounds it; and a pervasive belief that it is the key to success weights it with import. It has become a lightning rod in recent years due to world economic conditions and the loss of profitable blue-collar careers. Parents and schools experience pressure to prepare teenagers specifically for college entrance, and often the way in which this preparation manifests runs counter to what science has shown us is healthy or productive for the developing adolescent brain.

Our genes can be turned on and off by environmental toxins. Fast food, smoking, alcohol, drugs, dehydration and viral infection can cause mutations in genetic sequencing, genetic deficits that can lead to hard wiring defects. Epigenetic abnormalities during critical periods can cause genes not to work. Stress and lack of sleep, the hallmarks of the contemporary high school experience for the college-bound, can alter gene expression. Muir brings cutting-edge science to the parents of the teenagers she counsels about college admissions, and now to the parents of any teenager. In the next pages she provides an overview of the brain, explains why teenagers are often considered difficult and discusses the implications of epigenetics and neuroscience on the age-old practice of rearing children and getting them into college. The message of *Live Wires* is cautionary, and shows that neuroscience offers hope. Examining and making necessary changes to our lifestyle can have a biological effect on our teenagers and improve their lives. Muir's work—though it flies in the face of many of our current practices, provides plenty of optimism.

As Muir beautifully describes, there are indeed both nature and nurture—or genes and environment. Human interactions, learning and repetition, and kindness and nurturing can inform gene expression in the brain, the consequence being the transformation of an individual. With the proper environmental influences, a recalcitrant or rebellious adolescent can transform into a mature and successful young adult.

In *Live Wires* Muir uses these principles of genetics, brain circuitry and plasticity to weave a story that is filled with hope—a story that is the beginning of a new enlightenment. With this sentinel publication, an old story is being told by a masterful teacher who has meshed the time-honored principles of child rearing and education with the powerful new scientific data and insights that are emerging from the burgeoning field of neuroscience.

Is adolescence too late to improve an individual's chances for a successful life? *Live Wires* will bring a sigh of relief from harried high school teachers and a glimmer of hope for the parents who worry each day that their sons and daughters are incapable of living up to their potential. Now there is scientific evidence to validate the importance of their hard work and even greater reason to persevere no matter what the odds. I tend to think that these individuals, so dedicated to teenagers' success, already knew the answer. How satisfying for them to have this insightful reinforcement.

Gerard T. Berry, M.D.
Professor of Pediatrics
Harvard Medical School

Chapter
/ 01
YOUR
GENES
DO NOT HAVE
TO BE YOUR
DESTINY

The End of the Nature vs. Nurture Debate

Parents and educators through the last few decades have watched the Nature vs. Nurture debate as if it were a tennis match. When researchers like Arnold Gesell indicated that children were "just born that way" and would develop in their own good time, parents breathed a collective sigh of relief, and enjoyed or disciplined or despaired their children without guilt. When later studies showed that nurture played the key role in a child's success or failure, sales of "Baby Einstein" videos soared—data now shows why they did not always work as anticipated—and enrollment in enrichment classes increased dramatically. Back and forth the debate has raged, both sides often citing flawed or misleading research, with parents and teachers alike getting confused, eventually sticking with one champion or just forging ahead the best way they could with their education and experience.

Well, the Brain Open is finally over, and after several grueling matches, science has declared a tie. It's Love All, and Nature and Nurture are both contenders. We are born with genes; our experiences shape how the genes express or repress. That's just the way it is. Neither side of the court was exactly right.

Nurture was correct in that the way we shape our family environments can nurture the experiences that trigger genetic expression to ignite brain development in our precious children. The more we understand about the environments we are creating for our children, the more we can maximize their future options. Nature was right in that the genes we are born with are what we have to work with, but that point of view didn't take into account the relationship between nature and nurture. The most exciting thing brain science has discovered—and the observation that most informs the old debate—is this: **First we create our environments. Then, in turn, our environments generate the experiences that create us.**

The other longstanding debate regarding the optimal way to rear and educate children concerns the "Window of Opportunity." What Tiger Mother hasn't heard that if her child hasn't mastered violin by age three, it's pointless to take up the instrument? Brain science's exciting new breakthroughs point out that we can continue enhancing our environments and recreating ourselves throughout our lives. Your teenager is not a *fait accompli*. By understanding the implications of brain structure and development, you can still help your teenager to achieve optimal brain flourish. **It is never too late to make changes and get better results.** But it is important to understand your teen's brain to know when to accelerate and when to slow down. The current frenzy about achievement can compromise our kids' health.

Why Me?

I didn't plan to write a book. But my grandmother always told me that the called are never prepared, and the prepared are never called. When we find ourselves introduced to an extraordinary understanding or teaching, we have to share the information we have been given. Through my searching to find answers to my own questions, I have been exposed to teachers, mentors, students, and parents who have given me an exciting wealth of information about brain development and how it can be enhanced through proper understanding and care. I am compelled to share it.

Here's how my search started: I was a mother of three grown children; a grandmother to eight babies, toddlers, and young children; and the daughter of a wonderful woman who was starting to lose her way cognitively. Through my experiences rearing my own children plus my work over three decades with over 2,500 teens as a former head of school, director of college counseling and a high-powered internship program for seniors, I had a deep, intuitive belief that families who actively channeled their children in what my grandmother would have called "healthy ways" had children who were more successful in school and in life.

When my husband Rob and I were young parents, we spent hours reading to our children, exploring historic places, and setting up elaborate holiday treasure hunts to pique their curiosity. We tried to maintain a regular bedtime; we took their questions seriously; we encouraged them to be good friends; and we didn't let them eat junk—at least not too often. We didn't do these things so they could get into the college of their choice; we did them because that was good parenting. Back then, parenting wasn't as goal-oriented as it has become in the competitive, digital world we find ourselves in now.

Needless to say, with my professional experience layered on my parenting experience, I had opinions about how our daughters and our son should rear our grandchildren. Knowing that the three of them were intelligent people with their own firmly held beliefs and knowing that they were independent thinkers—as their father and I had hoped they would be—I knew I couldn't just tell them how to handle our grandchildren. At the same time, I was caring for both my husband's mother and my mother, each of whom was battling the physical and cognitive ravages of aging.

I began to notice that the structure—the pattern of life—that was most beneficial for our aging mothers was also what I most wanted to advocate to our children for their young families—for themselves, too. Through my work, I was reading about the breakthroughs that were happening in brain science. I began reading more deeply, getting more fascinated and, I suspect, becoming more opinionated about the incredible insight science was providing us about the brain and the applications I saw for parents, educators, communities, even cultures. Hardly a family gathering passed when I wasn't quoting Bruce McEwen and his research on the negative effects of stress on our long-term health or John Ratey on the importance of exercise which pumped oxygen to our brain—the cognitive candy it craves for efficiency!

Finally, I realized that what had begun as loosely organized continuing education, applied as kitchen science to my own family, had become something more to me. I wanted to understand these breakthroughs in depth. Rob was shocked when I told him I had applied and been accepted to yet another graduate program in Mind, Brain, and Education at Harvard University because I wanted to become a discerning consumer and wade through the probable pop science and past the charismatic presenters to dig into the real neuroscience research so we could figure out how to enrich the quality of life for our two mothers and to ensure rich development for our eight grandchildren. In retrospect, while he was shocked, he might not have been surprised since I had done this to him once before when our own children were young.

I had a mentor: John Cooper, a remarkable headmaster of a prominent independent school in Houston. At his request, for a full year I had homeschooled a teenage girl who had lost her way, followed by yet another teenage girl who had derailed, then a teenage boy who was manifesting memory lapses—we later discovered he had been smoking pot in his car during lunch breaks. I pummeled Mr. Cooper with probing questions, as both a new mother who did not want her own children to face a similarly disenfranchised adolescence and as a nascent educator who was desperate to know how to help these teens find their way. He modeled for me what would become my way of life: he picked up the phone and went to the best sources of the day, at that time the Gesell Institute of Child Development at Yale, and said he was sending me up to study with them. Surely, he said, there must have been something we could have done earlier in these teens' lives to position them to weather the storms of adolescence with more positive resolve. So, three decades later, when I had the probing questions about brain regression triggered by our mothers and about brain development prompted by our grandchildren, it was just logical that I go to Harvard, notably the current seat of cutting-edge research in the emerging field of modern neuroscience investigating the architecture of brain development.

I have great respect for tradition, and I believe families are the torch-bearers of tradition. I also believe that the opposite of growth is death. If we cannot adapt to new environments, we are doomed. We find ourselves at the beginning of a new century, a new millennium. Life is changing faster than any of us can understand. What I learned at Harvard about the brain and how it affects the developing child gives me hope on a personal level: hope for my grandchildren, hope for me as a person wanting to maximize my experience on this planet, and hope for all of the children we are preparing today to live in an age of technology and rapid change.

What Brain Science Can Mean for Your Teen

Perhaps more importantly for you, the understanding I have gained gives hope that your teenager—who seems to confound you at every turn, who seems to have no concept that he is not the peak and purpose of evolution, who seems to have forgotten the definition of risky— is in fact on the right track. The very same teenager who can get involved in video games for endless hours is also the teenager who can explain a book she read in English in a way that makes you see your own life with new eyes, or volunteer in the heat and humidity to build houses, teach camp, provide food or otherwise help people in such different circumstances than hers. And there are practices you can build into your family life to maximize that amazing—if undeniably frustrating—young person's ability to have the most rewarding life possible.

My research and experience have left me in awe of the amazing teen brain. I will share my paradigm shift with you in the following pages and demonstrate how to guide your teen to greatness—igniting his brain to maximize his own personal potential—with a few simple, but strategic, shifts in your mindset and environment. These shifts are easy to make, but so easy to miss, if you do not understand why they are imperative to your teen.

Circumstance conspired with curiosity to put me in the position of being exposed to information that can change your family dynamic in ways that will most optimize your children's ability to fully explore the potential of their genetic promise. *Genes load the gun; experience pulls the trigger.* As a mother, grandmother, and educator, I would be remiss if I didn't share this exciting new science with you.

Neuro-Parenting Principles
CHAPTER ONE

1. Nature through Nurture

2. Experience shapes brain development.

3. It is never too late to change.

4. Change the question if you want
   a better answer.

5. Mentors seed teens passion for finding purpose.

6. Neuroscience can help you guide
   your teen to his own personal greatness.

7. You can enhance your own genetic
   expression through experience.

BRAIN
BASICS

Getting Grounded in the Neural Lightning
Storm in Your Teen's Brain

BRAIN BIO 101

Your Brain Wires What It Experiences. Neurons are the electrically charged cells that populate your brain. Boasting one hundred trillion connections between neurons, your brain is a remarkably complicated network.

Your brain is an energy hog. Three pounds of Jell-0®, with a little tapioca thrown in, your brain uses twenty percent of your energy to jolt electrical messages across the hundreds of miles of wire that comprise your central nervous system. Neurons pick up signals through your sensory channels—seeing, hearing, smelling, tasting, touching—and transmit messages with lightning speed.

Your brain is ruthlessly efficient, working through associations, connecting every new input to something in the past, trying to decide what to do in response to the sensory signal it has just received.

Your brain's primary function: survival! Does the dark shadow bode harm, the crackle scream out an attacker, the smoke mean fire, the bitterness signal poison, the heat warn of a burn? The fight or flight response is your brain's most important job. Everything your brain does relates to this function, and much of it is done subconsciously, based on past experience.

We have always believed that early life experiences matter, but now research explains how these lightning storms of neural activity result in physical changes to our brains that impact future learning, health, and productivity.

Our brain builds these neural connections rapidly at first; then it prunes away the ones it thinks it won't need. Our brain overproduces, preparing for anything the world might offer. A brain hedges its bets. At birth, for instance, your baby's brain has the capacity to learn and to speak any speak any language in the world. It takes in the sounds of the people talking, the context into which it is born. A brain differentiates sounds, then it prunes the connections it does not need. Over time, your child's brain diminishes in its capacity to differentiate and reproduce sounds. A brain overproduces, then prunes for efficiency, a pattern it follows across sensory systems, across time.

By age one, your baby's brain is already pruning language and sensory pathways—defying those who might suspect that little is happening inside that emerging infant head. In fact, a lot is going on in there!

NEURAL NETWORK

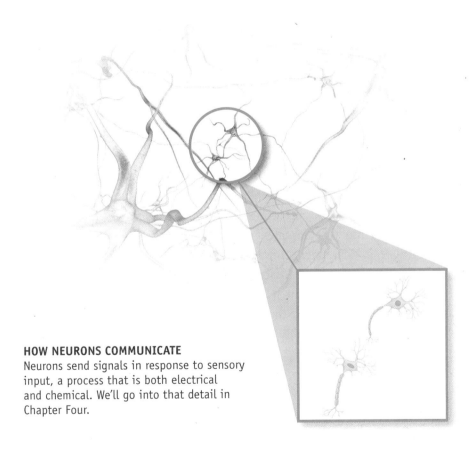

HOW NEURONS COMMUNICATE
Neurons send signals in response to sensory input, a process that is both electrical and chemical. We'll go into that detail in Chapter Four.

Nature Through Nurture: New Knowledge backed up by neuro-science data confirms that brain development occurs through the interaction of genes and experience and that children learn best in meaningful relationships.

Three Neuro-Parenting Principles to Ignite Your Teen's Brain

1. **Building Responsive Relationships.** Supportive relationships and positive learning experiences begin at home. A brain is looking for positive, responsive interactions wherever it can find them. Children learn best in meaningful relationships, which will prepare them for later success in school, the workplace, personal relationships, and the community. The clock is ticking in brain development. Seven hundred connections between neurons—synapses—per second will be made on a preset biological schedule, for good or bad.

2. **Mitigating Toxic Stress.** Changing demands in our current culture induce unprecedented stressors: longer work hours to achieve aggressive goals and perceived material needs; lack of support from the business community to align work schedules to children's needs; geographic isolation of extended family support systems, often landing children in daycare from infancy or with nannies who may not be equipped to meet a child's needs. We all have more trouble balancing our career and family responsibilities because the sheer velocity of the current century hurls the cultural furniture around, sometimes turning it to junk. In addition, current achievement mania and unbearable expectations are putting our kids under screws at the worst time in their development. The college application process alone can become an amplifier, morphing challenge into threat, potentially activating the stress response system, which can lead to long-term health compromises for certain vulnerable teens. There is much you can do within this microcosm to keep your teen healthy as you catapult him to his maximum potential!

3. **Managing the Positive Potential of Media.** How do we prepare the digital brains that populate our classrooms for the global world they will enter? We can learn from gamers who persist in the face of failure.

The average teen logs more than 10,000 hours of media, fewer than 10,000 hours in the classroom. Media opens up opportunities to learn from masters and explore topics not previously accessible. It can provide a digital spark to ignite a teen brain, and it has the potential to seed passion, leading teens to their own purpose and direction.

Relationships. Stress. Media. Three dangerously familiar words that we think we understand. Yet they contain the hidden curriculum, the ingredients for the secret sauce that parents need to move teens to their own personal greatness. These three words, when properly understood and applied, can be the levers that tip biology in your teen's favor, that ignite your teen's passion.

Meeting Developmental Needs of Children

When we know early experiences are wired into our children's brains, into their nervous systems, we cannot simply turn our backs and walk away. Biological processes interact chemically with environmental influences and affect complex behaviors such as attention, self-regulation and adaptive response. Environment and relationships combine to meet the needs of developing children by forging the foundation—weak and wobbly or strong and resilient—for subsequent cognitive and behavioral growth.

Three Tenets Stand Out

1. **Emotion**, whether a child feels safe or threatened, **determines cognitive progress or collapse.**
2. **Growth happens in bursts and regressions; it is seldom linear.** Normal is only a setting on a washing machine!
3. **Children are wired to learn through exploration**. Providing children with tools for self-regulation and conflict resolution starts early.

Children can have different experiences in the same environment, the same family. Take siblings, for example. An aggressive child will elicit different responses from a parent than a passive child might, and each will be influenced differently by the other. So environments can affect children in different ways, shaped by the relationships, circumstances and personal response patterns of each individual.

In the following pages, I will translate the science, investigate the issues, and change the questions we must ask to assure healthy brain development for our children. As you move through this book, you will discover how you can ignite your own child's brain development—how you can get it right from the start or how you can make it better from where you are right now. Let's look at what the amazing teen brain can do, then reflect on what it takes to get your child there, how to stay healthy in the process, and how to survive the stressful college application process. My goal for your family is that you love each other from the start of the journey to the end!

Neuro-Parenting Principles
CHAPTER TWO

1. Early lessons stick.
2. Your brain connects each new experience to a past experience for efficiency.
3. Your brain does everything in context.
4. Your brain is wired to keep you safe by responding to sensory signals.
5. Learning happens in meaningful relationships.
6. Emotion sets the tone for learning to happen.
7. Everyone grows differently, on his or her own developmental time schedule.
8. Children learn through experiences.

THE
AMAZING
TEEN
BRAIN

L et's look more closely at some teenagers and let them tell us what really ignites their brains. What does the latest brain science research mean for them, these adolescents whose brains have been developing and differentiating for over a dozen years? Their brains have experienced infancy, early childhood, young childhood. They have been nurtured at home, usually at schools, and often in camps, teams, classes, and other extra-curricular experiences. Their brains have some mileage on them, and they reflect the way they have been treated. Society often scoffs at the teenage brain, and there are many stereotypes associated with the behaviors of adolescents. I have a different take on the subject, and I believe you will, too, after you read their insightful comments. We'll go deeper into the science in Chapter Four.

Learning from Interns

For each of the past twenty-five years, I have been guiding over one hundred high-school seniors to three-week January internships strategically planned for good fit and personal growth, internships that match the student's aptitudes and interests. Over one hundred interns a year times twenty-five years has provided me with more than 2,500 stories about what happens when a teen walks out of a classroom and into a boardroom, newsroom or operating room. These experiences trigger enhanced expression of a student's genetic potential.

Here's what some of them have to say about the effect of their experience. We'll start with John, who worked with a cardiovascular surgeon:

> *I peered at the carefully arranged array of tools and materials on the table before me, wondering how so many different items are required for just one surgery. Minutes later I watched the scalpel trace a thin line down the patient's sternum. After a few deft maneuvers by the surgeon, I gazed upon the beating heart of another human being. Observing open-heart surgery for the first time was definitely one of the most memorable things I have done in my life. With every procedure I watched, I was constantly blown away by the miracle of modern medicine and how it is possible to open a human being up—like the hood of a car—to make repairs.*

John's experience is representative of the growth I have observed over the years through internship experiences. While students discovered the nuances of professional roles, they also discovered a great deal about themselves and catapulted their own learning, clarifying potential college majors and future career paths. Science confirms that students learn best in meaningful relationships, the hallmark of internships.

Interestingly, teens' vulnerability can become their secret weapon. Teens get a lot of perplexed press about the way they make decisions, a plethora of comments pointing to the later development of the prefrontal cortex—the seat of judgment and reason, and the last part of the brain to develop. Ironically, what makes teens most vulnerable may just be what makes them most malleable for preparation for the adult life that awaits them. I have witnessed learning that shocks teachers, who marvel at what a teen is capable of internalizing on location, through meaningful relationships, with projects that are relevant.

Sheridan, another intern, followed a pediatric cardiovascular surgeon and showed how a teen can change her brain to meet the experience at hand:

> *I read* Comprehensive Surgical Management of Congenital Heart Disease *to learn about basic heart anatomy so I could understand what normally happens before beginning to tackle complex defects and their surgical repairs. Whenever I read or heard a new vocabulary word I looked it up on Wikipedia so I could understand the surgeries I was lucky enough to see each day. I learned about deoxygenated blood flow, the superior and inferior vena cavas, tricuspid valves, pulmonary artery, mitral valve, arterial switch procedure to correct a dextrotransposition of the great arteries, Tetralogy of Fallot—another congenital disease. The first day in the operating room I was clueless, but with the help of this textbook, I began to understand and be in awe of the daily procedures and the remarkable medical team that performed these life-saving surgeries.*

Teens are getting smarter. But the learning platform is changing with transformative technology and the information explosion at hand. Look at Sheridan's learning curve. My friend Dr. David Eagleman, a neuroscientist at Baylor College of Medicine, would describe Sheridan's quest as "just-in-time learning"—she needed the vocabulary to build context and link new information, and she needed it right then. Given that content is now readily available on the Web, she found what she needed!

"Just-in-time learning" sticks, unlike "just-in-case learning"—the kind that classrooms often provide, the amorphous lecture the brain holds until after a test on that unit. Dr. Eric Mazur, professor of physics at Harvard, speaks convincingly about "The Twilight of the Lecture." He originally thought that if he taught, kids learned; over his years of teaching, he came to realize the fallacy rooted in his assumption. His take on "active learning" is challenging the style of teaching that has ruled universities for 600 years. Mazur demonstrates that when projects are relevant and interactive, students learn.

Getting Inside the Teen Brain

In order to prepare our students for the world they will enter, perhaps we should be focusing more frequently on making them discerning consumers. We should teach them how to use their digital devices effectively and how to distinguish reliable sources, instead of making them keep their smart devices in their pockets or their lockers while at school. Education is at the cusp of change. The teacher is no longer the purveyor of all knowledge. Even the best of schools may be running on the inertia of their historical reputations, instead of leading with best practices based on cutting-edge research that documents how students learn best.

This new crop of digital learners who populate our homes and classrooms today will change the way we think about education, just as the latest brain science changes the way we should look at teenagers. In order to understand adolescents, we need to understand their brains.

Teenagers' brains are programmed to receive sensory information, interpret it, and then respond to it appropriately, all within the cultural expectations of a teen's world. A teen brain consists of over 100 billion neurons, functioning in interconnected networks, coded into more than fifty neurotransmitter molecules—all of which function collaboratively to move information through their brain to regulate their body as it interacts with the complex world. Parts of the brain develop sequentially, but not simultaneously; this is the reason adolescence can be confusing.

Here's the issue: the later part of the brain to develop, the prefrontal cortex, controls judgment, self-regulation, and deferred gratification. Dealing with these developing qualities can trip some teens, sometimes. "How-to-do-it" matures before "whether-to-do-it." Teen brains also have to figure out how to read other's intentions, so social and cultural stimulation further confound the developing brain. And the brain works smart, so it ties every new encounter to a past experience. However, it might not pull out the right file as it edits and re-files the experience. This jumbled filing system allows room for confusing behaviors as a teen works to get all parts of a growing brain working in sync.

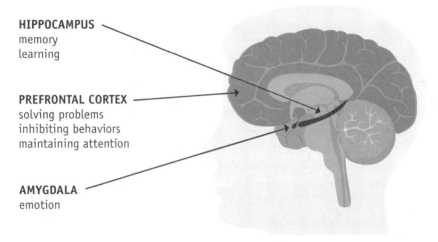

HIPPOCAMPUS
memory
learning

PREFRONTAL CORTEX
solving problems
inhibiting behaviors
maintaining attention

AMYGDALA
emotion

Through their study, work, games and play, adolescents are practicing, preparing for adult challenges ahead. All the while they are strengthening needed connections among neural networks and eliminating unneeded connections, developing the capacity to respond reflectively over time.

Since a developing brain is only about two percent of a teen's body but uses twenty percent of a teen's energy, sleep and nutrition are of utmost importance. Most teens need nine hours of sleep a night, but many get between four and seven hours. What does this mean? They are living with constant jet lag! Glycogen, the stored form of glucose that is the brain's energy source, can only be replenished during inactive periods. During sleep, sensorimotor activity stops but brain activity does not. Sleep can shape emotional response, keeping it appropriate—or not, if sleep deprivation persists.

The Relationship Between Emotion and Learning

Recent research from Antonio Damasio and Mary Helen Immordino Yang, renowned neuroscientists from the University of Southern California, is rich with empirical data confirming that emotion drives learning. Their findings support my observations in the internship program. Even as teens are demonstrating mastery of material at higher levels, retaining transient facts—facts that may be fleeting over time—long enough to perform well on achievement tests, I see deep emotion emanating from teens as they build relationships. Alicia's account of her internship experience in an orphanage in Honduras reveals how teens can learn and then navigate emotion, discovering how their own baseline experiences may shape their responses differently from children whose early experiences were not the same. Sometimes the different tracks lead to surprising results. Alicia learned that early experiences shape whether a child sees the world as friendly or hostile:

> *I had made the assumption that girls who had been abandoned would accept love and compassion. But what I learned was that they sometimes build walls around their hearts in self-defense and have a hard time trusting others. I experienced charity in which you get nothing in return—often no gratitude or appreciation. But you keep on loving and helping anyway because you know they need it.*

Ah, beautiful teen brains!

Experience Shapes the Brain

So what is going on in those mysterious teen brains that worries parents and confuses teachers? Alongside the biological development of the brain itself, consider the cultural overlay: educational and economic determinants cause children to remain dependent longer than in the past. Humans have a longer period of dependence than any other primates. Adolescence is a creation and byproduct of our culture, unique to our species.

Children used to have cultural experiences under the supervision of adults—hunters and gatherers went out with fathers, and nurturers and caregivers remained with their mothers—to practice those tasks. According to Dr. Alison Gopnik, professor of psychology at the University of California, Berkeley, children started their internships at seven, not at twenty-seven as they often do today. We've all heard the phrase "extended adolescence" used to describe the many bright young adults who remain exuberant but refrain from commitment to a particular career path or relationship until well into their thirties.

So, following Gopnick's research, experience shapes the brain. Yet, the brain is powerful precisely because it is so sensitive to experience. For example, as Gopnik indicates, practice forces development, shaping the circuits in the prefrontal cortex. Remember, this is the area that helps teens manage their impulses. Simultaneously, the experience of working to control impulsive behaviors during practice helps the prefrontal cortex develop what teens need for controlling their impulsive behaviors. Thus, life experiences shape our biology.

These experiences actually get into the biology of our bodies, laying the foundation for future productivity and health. These experiences shape the people we become. Genes are just the beginning, the first step. Their interaction with the environment will determine individual outcome. In order to develop and function effectively, the prefrontal lobes—the control center of a teenager—need to be exercised and instructed. This adage about exercise and instruction applies to children of all ages, of course.

A Porsche Engine with Model T Brakes

Dr. Ronald Dahl, developmental pediatrician and sleep researcher at the University of California, Berkeley, speaks of teens as having a Porsche engine with Model T brakes. He points to the common sense needed in rearing teens. One way to apply his wisdom could be thinking about the way we have nascent teen drivers learn under supervision. Teens build skill, moving toward mastery through a gradual system. At first they would have no peers in the car, to minimize distractions. This process works well because—surprising to many teens, as well as to their adult parents—the brain cannot multi-task. For example, automobile safety stats confirm that driving while texting slows down response time to 1.7 seconds; response time is 1.4 seconds when driving drunk! Not only do we need to provide teens with guidance, but it also has to follow a progression. And, as teens are building skills, we need to determine if we are dealing with their full attention or a fraction of their capacity.

Increasing Relevance through Internships

We keep giving our teens more class time and more homework, all with good intentions, of course. Other countries show greater progress in certain disciplines; we are fearful that our students won't stand up to the rigors of selective college admissions. We want them to have the ability to live the best life possible. Yet research shows us that more homework and longer hours in the classroom may not be the most effective means to achieve mastery and competence. What other options do we have?

My experience with interns suggests that we should consider more field experience and more project-based classrooms for our teens. Science now confirms that students learn best in meaningful relationships with adults who make lessons relevant and interactive, the hallmarks of an internship. Don't worry: I'm not advocating a move away from formalized education. We still need teachers and schools. But let's look at some of the ways the following interns benefited from their field experience.

Mike had an experience in his senior internship that caused him to understand the concept of meaningful work. His realization illustrates how our brains function to build a sense of social conscience and environmental awareness.

> Before my internship, I wanted to be a petroleum engineer because I thought it would be fun—like being a modern day treasure hunter. Afterwards, I realized that understanding the energy industry was a moral responsibility for me to help the United States economy become more stable by being less dependent on foreign energy.

Natasha and Joe both witnessed the importance of collaboration in their internships. Natasha gained an understanding of the team play involved in surgery.

> My internship revealed the complex network of team players that harmonize to form a community of caretakers who aim to serve and to heal. Standing no more than four feet away from a patient, I witnessed the pages of my textbook come alive, jump out, find new meaning. From neurosurgery and craniotomies, to plastic surgery and abdominoplasties— I was able to observe a pastiche of specialties and procedures.

"I witnessed the pages of my textbook come alive, jump out, find new meaning."

Isn't that what we want for our teenagers' education?

Joe's experience in an office opened his eyes in the same way. He explained:

I became aware of problems I never knew existed. I learned that the way to thrive is to listen to the customers and that in a successful office everyone does everything. I discovered that it is an immensely competitive world.

Teens can assume remarkable levels of responsibility. Should we ever doubt that teens are capable? Read what Michael had to say after his experience at a naval testing facility:

The first part of my work at the naval testing facility was with a mechanical engineer, who taught me to use a computer program that enabled me to reverse engineer an instrumentation board that needed to be put into a palette for an F-18 aircraft. This program was amazing— efficient and fast. But most of my time I spent in the hangar or on the flight line. I got to sit in four different aircraft and load software onto their systems. The only way to do this is to power up the plane, turn on the avionics and other instruments and load it from the cockpit. I got to sit in the cockpit and turn on the switches and push the different buttons. I actually sat alone in an F-18 cockpit that was fueled and ready for take-off. In addition, I changed the video recorders located behind the ejection seat. This task really scared me because in order to reach the equipment, I had to maneuver into the area behind the seat where the explosives were located that could blow open the canopy to release the ejection seat. While I was in the hangar, I removed and added various kinds of equipment from the aircraft, work which became somewhat routine after a few days. I learned a great deal about engineering, security, and fighter planes. I only wish I could have stayed longer!

Peer Pressure Can Be Risky Business

The odyssey through adolescence is fraught with emotionally charged moments where teens must make decisions, hopefully positive ones that leave them safe. Teens are inherently social. They seek validation, at this stage more from their peers than from the adults in their lives. This focus on their friends is appropriate: they are getting ready to individuate, to leave their family nest and move into an adult world where they will need to relate successfully with their peers. Because they seem to worry more about what their friends will think than listening to the advice of their parents, teens are often labeled, perhaps too quickly, sometimes too harshly, as underestimating risk. Let's look at that more closely.

B.J. Casey, professor of developmental psychobiology at Cornell University, says that research from MRI studies is suggesting that maybe teens overestimate reward, that reward simply trumps the potential for risk. Research conducted by Laurence Steinberg at Temple University suggests that perhaps the real issue is simply that the reward system lights up more when a peer is looking on during an experience. Peer pressure, which can produce either validation or rejection, may lead to more risk-taking behaviors. We'll look more at the specifics of this process and the role dopamine plays in Chapter Four. But for now, just know that peer pressure is a real, chemical thing in a teen's life.

Creative vs. Rebellious

Neurobiology is helping us understand how adolescents are moving toward adulthood. New research is at once both comforting and alarming, for even though we might understand more, it does not mean we can control better. I have come to think of teens as creative, rather than rebellious.

Some of our culture's finest discoveries have popped out of young minds that contradicted current trends: the young Charles Darwin, Albert Einstein, and James Watson come to mind with their scientific discoveries in biology and physics. My husband reminded me of a touching story about Thomas Edison during his youth. His mother needed surgery after dark, and the doctor asked him to gather as many lanterns as possible; in addition to the lanterns, Edison decided to hang mirrors along the walls to amplify the light instead of having it drift into the shadows. Lucky mother! Viewing teens through the lens of creativity, rather than rebellion, allows us to shift from trying to control to trying to mentor. Many productive adults, successful by most definitions, share that they had a mentor who encouraged them, who believed in them even before they believed in themselves.

Mentoring takes many forms. It centers on respect and the intent to unlock potential. It can be an informal camaraderie between a student and a like-minded teacher, or it can be formalized and include goal setting. If your teen's school has an internship program, I encourage you to look into it. Internships can offer a vehicle to guide this developmental passage by helping teens understand themselves better, even as they try to decipher their role in the adult world they are getting revved up to enter, and to investigate a meaningful career where they could be productive. And if your school has no formal program, businesses in many sectors are responsive to teens' serious inquiries about internships.

On their journey of self-discovery, teens look for clues about themselves, about what they should study in college. Alexis even found value in sorting the mail during her internship:

> While I sorted through piles of fan mail and lifted shipments of soda cans, I also learned the factors that go into a truly incredible script, how to create an acting reel, and how to read character breakdowns. I now know how certain actions translate on camera. I also made valuable friendships, while translating this industry to meet my future goals.

And in learning keyboard commands to be able to help in an architecture office, Kate found a professional goal.

> I dug into SketchUp and AutoCAD, learning keyboard shortcuts and new commands as quickly as possible so I could transfer designs onto SketchUp. I realized architecture will be a perfect match for me.

Parents can also help teens on their journey of self-discovery. I often advise parents to take their kids to work. Not only does it allow the teen to see the parent in another light, it provides an opportunity to discuss something unrelated to the teen's behavior. Taking responsibility for helping with an aspect of a parent's work—sorting files, making spread sheets, entering data, doing Internet research—validates teenagers' developing sense of self.

Fluid Intelligence

The Stehlin Foundation for Cancer Research tells me candidly that one reason they take on interns is because they anticipate that teens using fluid intelligence could very well see connections that their scientists might miss—a testament to the plasticity of the amazing teen brain!

Lou's experience confirms this:

> I have done a wide variety of tasks: "splitting cells;" running DNA gel electrophoresis; working with plasmid DNA—cutting out a length of base pairs of nucleotides, which make up a protein that causes cancer, and replacing it with an insert that would ensure that the sequence of nucleotides that made that protein would stop replicating.

What about Camp?

I gently nudge teens away from summer camp experiences, depending on how many years they might have attended. Repeating an experience may not be as apt to promote the personal growth that results from getting out of your comfort zone and tackling the unknown. Vygotsky described the "Zone of Proximal Development" as the sphere where deep learning transpires: where challenge trumps comfort, but where fear does not morph into cognitive collapse. That zone of proximal development is what parents seek and what teachers value, even without necessarily understanding the impact on a growing brain. Summer jobs and internships with real responsibility shape brain development that can translate to positive outcome.

Irena interned at a television station. She went from working at the assignment desk to working with reporters on breaking stories. Here's how she describes the experience:

> Police radios and buzzing phones added noise to an already crazy place. Reporters showed me how to find important parts of an interview, how to write a package, and how to edit to prepare a package for the news. I learned how stories to be covered are chosen and how producers fit together a newscast. I met people who were willing to teach me as much as I was willing to learn.

That's a far cry from making s'mores, and the experience enabled her to stretch and develop in new ways.

Evidence abounds about how quickly teens can learn. Kelly interned on a trading desk and gained enough information about stocks, bonds and options to interact with brokers.

I studied the process of trading stocks, bonds, and options. My days began at 5:30 a.m. so I could be included in the morning conference calls where analysts make their daily forecasts. The frenetic pace included focused research for portfolio reviews, daily reading of the news that could affect the market, and frequent phone interaction with brokers calling in with questions.

Teens consistently rise to the occasion when the projects are relevant; then brain plasticity takes over!

The Value of Vacations

And what of family vacations? Too good to waste! What an opportunity to build family relationships and pass along family values. Consider family service—saving sea turtles, cleaning up the parks with forest rangers, monitoring the habitat of wolves being reintroduced to Yellowstone, an archeological dig in Majorca. Or pursue independent research into family cultural backgrounds in a country of origin. Unpack the architectural and historic heritage of a city. Or perhaps language immersion through a mission trip to Costa Rica helping orphans learn to read. Children learn that there is more that connects us as a global community than divides us, a lesson that might just preserve our civilization and our economy.

Improved Learning Impacts College Admission

Relationships coupled with interactive and relevant just-in-time-learning episodes enrich a student's journey of self-discovery and become fodder for deeper college essays later. Rick Shaw, Dean of Undergraduate Admission and Financial Aid at Stanford, talks about the reason behind their final essay question: *What matters to you and why?* Shaw says that knowing what a senior is thinking about is what they really want to know when making an admit/reject decision.

Like many teen interns, Marshall saw beyond the obvious; he discovered basic human truths:

At the criminal district court, I saw plea deals ranging from stealing lingerie at Wal-Mart to identity theft and trials ranging from juvenile misdemeanors to capital murders. I have decided that many people could be good with proper guidance.

Skylar learned how valuable patience is in helping others:

Working in a second-grade classroom, I have discovered that when a place feels nurturing, safe, and supportive, it's the perfect environment for learning. I believe that reassurance is what makes students strive to be their best. I learned how to be patient when a child didn't understand and to find new ways to explain. I think devoting your time to working with children is a selfless job. It's making your life all about making other lives stand out and grow.

Experience shapes the journey. Experience crafts the story and connects the brain circuitry. Experience molds the person.

Yes, teens may make reckless decisions, but we need to focus our efforts and creative thought on how we can craft experiences to grow neural connections in their amazing brains. As children take on adult roles later due to their extended time in school, going even beyond college years into requisite graduate study or into extended adolescence, the importance of guiding them to interact with their world through meaningful relationships and experiences reverberates as a clarion call.

Extending the Classroom

Transformative technology allows us to push out the walls of a classroom and stretch learning across domains, across cities, states, even countries. We can find teachers everywhere through the Web. Will Richardson, who writes extensively about the value of the Web for learning, relates that his son was working on a project and reached out on the Internet to an expert in Scotland—who turned out to be an eleven-year-old boy with the right store of research and expertise for the project, as a result of his own previous investigation.

The Implications of Brain Plasticity

The ground-breaking research of Dr. Jay Giedd at the National Institute of Mental Health points to a second proliferation of neural growth during the teen years. Giedd alerts savvy parents and teachers to inform teens about this surge, guiding them to make smart choices, making teens aware of the scientific proof that they either *use it or lose it*. The brain prunes back the connections that are not activated through use, assuming it does not need these connections for survival. Adolescence is no time to be a couch potato, for sure!

Remember, the brain is an energy hog, pulling out twenty percent of a body's energy to get its job done. It has to work smart, and it is constantly adapting in ways it believes are better. Dr. Charles Nelson, pediatrician and professor of pediatrics at Harvard Medical School, points out how this aspect of the brain makes teens vulnerable. Brain plasticity can pattern addictive behaviors as the brain wires what it experiences. Science now confirms that alcohol and nicotine are more dangerous for a teen brain because they interfere with neurotransmitter receptor processes.

Dr. Jack Shonkoff, pediatrician and Director of Harvard's Center on the Developing Child, would be quick to assure teens that their prefrontal cortex is working hard to build the myelination—the insulation—that will make the transmission of electrical signals faster and more efficient through their central nervous system (more on that in Chapter Four). His message rein-forces how experience gets into our biology, for better or worse.

What does brain plasticity mean for us in regard to our teenagers? Guiding teens to positive experiences and rethinking how they learn, remember, respond, and assimilate new information is critical. Removing barriers to learning, which traditional classrooms and standard lecture formats can produce in abundance without realizing it, must be a point of serious review for educators.

When students spend more time in the classroom, they might become better scientists or historians, but they do not necessarily become better people or become better equipped to handle the adult world they will enter. Teens need to learn how to ask the probing questions that will solve the problems they'll encounter: Problems too big for one brain or one discipline, problems that will require collaboration and real teamwork. During this surge of neural growth, we need to provide opportunities to teens that can change their lives. As a result, they will have the capability to change our world.

Valuing Multiple Intelligences

After working with teens for well over two decades, I have discovered that there is more than one kind of intelligence, for sure. Thank goodness! I had colleagues once tell me that underperforming teens needed to earn the right to an internship, demonstrating their responsibility through a top academic profile. Bells and whistles went off in my head. That approach simply did not sit well with me.

I dug into empirical data to see what science might be telling me about adolescent brain development. I found Dr. Howard Gardner, who later became my adviser in my graduate program at Harvard. Gardner, a developmental psychologist, writes prolifically about multiple intelligences. I saw his research play out with my senior interns repeatedly. Many educators teach to, understand, and reward primarily one type of academic intelligence. This approach leaves kids who learn differently, those in the margins, questioning their abilities.

But what is good for the kids in the margins is good for all kids! Multiple means of representation in our classrooms, multiple means of assessment can reach multiple kinds of learners. Differentiation? It's as old as the one-room schoolhouse and as new as the neuroscience guiding us today. Science is confirming what we have always known: each kid is different, each kid is too important to lose. We need every one of them to make our economy strong and our culture flourish.

Think about the human capital perspective. Public records tell us it can cost $6,000 to remediate a student, $9,000 to retain a student for a year, and up to $125,000 to incarcerate a student we have failed in our school system. Dollars going to building prisons represent an enormous public expenditure. We can do better with our money, with our children. Science shows we have the ability to provide environments for our children that can improve their outcomes, throughout their development.

What Does It All Mean for These Amazing Teens?
We've touched on the challenges families face: changes in family structures and child care, economic forces that have sent both parents into the work force often leaving them less available, and geographic isolation among families. These additional burdens overlay the passage through adolescence that remains riddled with personal and family challenge.

This developmental passage profits from more direct supervision by experienced adults who can get teens into real-world problem solving. In addition, the trickle-down effect from the selective college admissions system rewards those teens who focus early and develop academic or artistic expertise. Many of these teens could be favorably served through enriching internships, strategically crafted and well-executed.

Families and schools need to see teens as creative rather than rebellious, and to provide opportunities for responsibility. Teens need to be valued for who they are and what they can eventually contribute, rather than just compared to a unilateral or bilateral academic yardstick. Most importantly, everyone involved with teens needs to understand that they are all about growth and change. If that growth is channeled in healthy ways, it can lead to increased genetic flourish and better outcomes for the teen. If it is not directed or if it is shut down, it can lead to ingrained destructive behaviors and teens will not come near to maximizing their potential. This second burst of neural growth during adolescence provides great opportunity.

That marvelous brain plasticity: experience can be a good teacher, after all, particularly when coupled with meaningful and relevant instruction. You heard it first from your grandmother, no doubt. Now science reminds us of her wisdom. Let's look further at healthy brain development and see if wisdom and science concur here as well.

Neuro-Parenting Principles
CHAPTER THREE

1. Teens learn best in meaningful relationships with projects that are relevant, the hallmark of good internships.

2. Teens need to become discerning consumers.

3. Healthy lifestyles for both brain and body incorporate adequate sleep and good nutrition.

4. Experience shapes the brain.

5. Paradigm shift: what the press labels as rebellion is also the valuable life trait creativity.

6. Use it or lose it—as a testament to brain plasticity, each experience changes the brain.

7. There is more than one kind of intelligence.

8. Mentors can ignite brain development during the second burst of neural growth during adolescence.

HEALTHY BRAIN
DEVELOPMENT

We've looked at some of the implications of the teenage brain, so let's back up and look more deeply at how those teenage brains have developed to that point. What does "healthy brain development" mean? Brain development starts at the very beginning of pregnancy. Dr. Charles Nelson, pediatrician and professor at Harvard Medical School—along with other prominent researchers—can now explain how brain development occurs with even more specificity. Billions of cells begin to form and then develop an intricate communication system; this process leads first to basic functions like seeing, hearing, and motor response and later, to more highly developed cognitive functions like reading and memory. Together, the components for healthy brain development are forming.

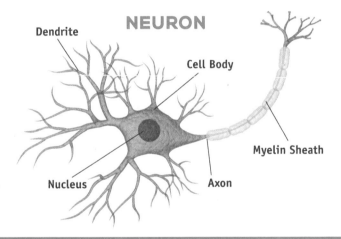

NEURON: specialized brain cell capable of sending and receiving information

DENDRITE: branches that capture incoming signals from other neurons

CELL BODY: largest part of neuron—contains nucleus

AXON: fiber bundle that carries signals away from cell body

MYELIN: insulation around some axons that increases speed of signals

NEUROTRANSMITTER: chemical used for communication between neurons

SYNAPSE: specialized site (small gap) for communication between neurons

Humans have about 100 billion neurons in their brain alone!

Cell Proliferation: Cells Grow and Communicate with Each Other

Nelson explains that during cell growth, called proliferation, neurons—the basic cell unit—and glia, which produce myelin, or insulation, form rapidly. Each neuron has a protruding axon that sends out signals and a profusion of branching dendrites that receive signals from other neurons. Neurons transmit an electrical pulse through the axon, and multiple dendrites receive the information. When axons and dendrites come together, a synapse is formed. Billions of cells are trying to communicate with each other. A circuit of connectedness is developing. Electrical transmission occurs when substances cross from one cell to another, moving information across cells in this systematic manner.

The brain rests in a saline solution inside the skull so these electrical impulses are moving through liquid. For efficiency, myelination wraps a fatty layer around the axons and dendrites—much like a wire is insulated—to speed up the connections and to keep them from short-circuiting in much the same way that we use plastic around copper wires in circuits in our house.

Cell Migration and Cell Specialization: Each Cell has a Special Job

Cell migration rushes these neurons to genetically determined destinations—Nelson likens this to passengers who have tickets to get off a train at designated stops—where they must begin their work to build their assigned segment of the brain. Cell specialization is in motion. Differentiation means that multiple areas of the brain are growing at the same moment. These cells must develop circuits with one another and become an efficient team to get their jobs done in the designated nine months allotted for the particularly protected period of intrauterine development.

Pruning: Cells That Are Not Used Disappear

The specialized cells are in place at birth. After birth, the focus shifts to building the connections into a highly integrated system of circuits.

The proliferation of synaptic connections between axons and dendrites becomes increasingly dense as dendrite arborization intensifies—much as a tree fills in its branches. Genes provide the cells and put them in place; experience grows the connections. Without the experience to reinforce a particular synapse as necessary, the brain gets rid of the circuit, assuming it will not be needed to function. Pruning is the brain's way of getting rid of what it thinks it will not need.

As we discussed in Chapter Three, adolescence is the time of maximum pruning. Pruning is based on experience. Therefore, experiences we provide our teens are just as critical as those we provide our babies, toddlers and young children. Remember the warning of Dr. Jack Shonkoff: *Use it or lose it!*

Neurotransmitters: Chemical Messengers Tell Cells to Turn Off or Turn On

Neurotransmitters carry the electrical signals from one cell to the other. Dopamine, serotonin, and acetocholene are frequent messengers in this process. These chemicals move through a key-and-lock system: the chemical unlocking the opening and passing through, followed by the lock closing down the opening. Whatever chemical remains after the lock-down is

THE NEUROTRANSMITTER DOPAMINE IN ACTION

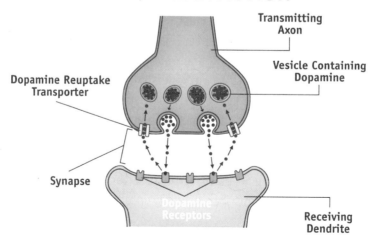

Transmitting Axon

Vesicle Containing Dopamine

Dopamine Reuptake Transporter

Synapse

Dopamine Receptors

Receiving Dendrite

reabsorbed. Bruce McEwen, noted for his research on stress—a topic we will cover in Chapter Five—recounts how drug interventions can block the reabsorption of chemicals like dopamine and serotonin. This process can alter moods by leaving these chemicals in the system longer. The brain's developing communication system is both structural and chemical. Todd Rose, educational neuroscientist at Harvard University, explains clearly to teens how certain drugs can affect the neurotransmitter system and interrupt healthy brain development.

Brain Plasticity—The Brain Reconfigures Itself Throughout Life Experience

Pruning is part of the normal progression. Pruning in the brain, just as in the plant world, is a means of becoming more efficient. An energy hog, the brain is always looking for ways to work smart. The timing of the pruning matters, and early experience matters even more. Nelson studied a piece of cortex from the brain which revealed that between birth and six years there is an exponential increase in the density of circuits; by fourteen years, the density is remarkably thinned out. This transformation results from experiences during sensitive—sometimes, critical—periods and the pruning of circuits not activated by experience.

For an infant to function—to see, to hear, to crawl, to walk, to climb—the brain is in high gear building circuits. Once a circuit is built, it cannot be rewired. But the miraculous brain has remarkable plasticity, which it carries throughout life. This plasticity allows the brain to work around a maladapted circuit that has already been put in place. But as Kurt Fischer, professor and Director of Harvard Graduate School of Education's Mind, Brain and Education program, explains, this process is harder—it takes more effort and is riskier—and may not work over time.

For instance, when improperly formed visual circuits are not corrected early, the prognosis for sight over time is less hopeful. The same relationship applies to early auditory dysfunction and later speech and language delays. Earlier intervention is certainly better than later; prevention is, of course, better than treatment; Shonkoff's research reassures us, however, that it is never too late for the brain to make adjustments.

Neuro-Parenting Principles
CHAPTER FOUR

1. Cells grow systematically, and then experience builds circuits.

2. Neurons communicate with each other through an electrical and chemical process.

3. Circuits that are not used are pruned away for efficiency.

4. Early experiences turn genes on.

5. ~~Once a circuit is wired, it cannot rewire,~~ but it can adapt.

6. Brain plasticity continues throughout life.

7. It is never too late to make adjustments.

DON'T
STRESS
ME OUT!

My husband and I have recently finished building our house. In the beginning, I watched the concrete take shape to form the foundation. Then the lumber went into place, and the house began to take shape. But out of sight, behind the walls and windows, were the pipes and wires, the less obvious supports that would render the end product successful—or not. I watched the magic of the connections built sequentially, not simultaneously, even as I anxiously eyed impending storms. I sensed that ill-timed rains could compromise fresh concrete or a half-finished portion of roof or even the raw materials piled high in the yard waiting to take a place in our home. A complication at the end could cause problems, too. We proved that when we were hanging the heavy mahogany signboard from the tanker my husband worked aboard and punctured a water pipe, spraying our freshly finished hardwood floors. We had to rip open sheet rock, go behind the wall, and dig into the hidden pipes to fix the unintended damage to our beautiful new home.

We had a new grandchild arrive as we started construction. Ebby's brain was growing in much the same manner, from the bottom up, dependent on sound connections. The promise of each new layer rested on the quality of the previous circuit, and the scaffolding had to hold steady for each new layer to develop. Basic circuits were wired, followed by more complicated circuits later: he had to develop sounds before he could learn words, which he could later use to form sentences. At any time, his developing circuitry could be vulnerable to storm damage: a virus, a fall, a faulty relationship, malnutrition, abuse.

Having seen my own children to adulthood, and having worked so intently to understand what I am conveying to you about amazing teenagers, I pondered this architecture of brain development in our grandson. How could we best protect him against the storms in his future? I worried about how we might inadvertently prick a hole in one of his vital sources of strength. What were our precious grandson's natural defenses against those moments when we, as a family, might simply be trying with good intentions to decorate his life with the signboards of our heritage and disrupt his wiring? What might natural and imposed stressors do to his brain development, his future health? How could we nurture young Ebby on his natural track—he can really throw a ball!

Thinking it over, I realized that two of the most important things to manage are stress and sleep. We'll look at how stress affects the brain here, and then look at sleep in Chapter Six.

What is Stress?

We feel stress when we feel out of control. Stress response is as individual as a fingerprint. Each of us reacts differently, based on the tools in our proverbial toolbox, the one that is filled with our early experiences and our own personal propensity for fear and anxiety. Remember, our brain is built for survival. It ratchets up the best of our biology when it feels threatened.

You now know that your child was born with most of the neurons he or she will have for life. Then the process of building circuits begins. These neural networks develop through interaction with people and environment. Genes are triggered by experience. Even the beginning signals—like crying or smiling—are interactive and are building the foundation of language through the sounds and actions.

Then a process of sculpting begins. I can't reiterate the message often enough: *use it or lose it*. Healthy circuits, the neural networks, build through stable relationships and rich learning experiences. Disruption of healthy brain circuitry during the crucial early years creates later complications in learning, behavior, and health. What does stress do to interrupt this process? Let's look at the biology of stress to see. And while we are examining the ways stress can ravage a precious baby, let's think about what it can do to our teenagers and to us, too.

The Effects of Stress on Our Body

Our stress response is set up to react in seconds to preserve our life from real or perceived threat. Our brains, hormones, and glands react immediately, rallying the oxygen, energy, and muscle power we need to either run or fight. Our heart, lungs, and blood go to work instantly for survival.

We've all felt this sudden surge of chemicals in our system. The scientific explanation comes from Bruce McEwen at Rockefeller University. Here's what this renowned neuroscientist discovered: your body picks up a sensory signal—a twig cracks in the dark, the smell of smoke—and the minute hypothalamus in your brain signals your adrenal gland, perched on the top of your kidney, to flood your system with adrenaline. Within seconds, you feel your pulse race, your blood pressure escalate, and you experience a surge of intense energy. You make an instant decision and react instinctively. You stand firm or run fast: the fight-or-flight stress response that you read about and see in action movies is happening to you!

Sometimes adrenaline is not enough. The next line of defense is for the adrenals to release cortisol. John Medina at the University of Washington, describes the release of cortisol as "the elite force," capable of knocking out the worst stressors and then returning us to baseline. As Medina points out, our ancestors either had to react in seconds or risk becoming a saber-toothed tiger's lunch. Our body is equipped to handle danger with a swift and efficient hand.

The Three Levels of Stress
Not all stress is bad for you. Some stress helps you do a better job, giving you the energy you need to focus and sustain.

Positive Stress. Young children experience a lot of stress. Separation anxiety starting preschool, denial of a request for a fifth cookie, shots at the doctor's office. Parents can deal with these stressors with consistent support. These stressors are considered positive because they lead to growth. Once a child determines preschool is a good place, all sorts of new opportunities await. For a teen, positive stress comes at the peak of learning or performing, when he still feels that, with persistence and focus, he has some kind of control over outcome.

Tolerable Stress. Illness. Hurricane Katrina. War. September 11, 2001. How successfully a child gets back to the baseline after stress depends on the supportive adult. Many of the same things create tolerable stress in young children also affect teenagers. Teens face the nagging perception of achievement, often dictated by their parents or their community. College applications, when tackled with the right spirit, can produce tolerable stress. That stress can be managed if a teen feels she has the support throughout the process of someone who believes in her and her abilities.

Toxic Stress. Strong, prolonged. Children facing toxic stress must have stable, predictable, reliable adults to bring them back to baseline. Without the predictable, supportive adult, the result is damage to brain architecture and the neural circuits. These kids develop a short fuse for stress response and are at high risk for health issues in adulthood. When challenge morphs into threat, toxic stress can occur.

The Science of Stress

Claude Bernard, a nineteenth-century French scientist, coined the term 'homeostasis' from the original Greek to describe our body's need to remain stable by staying the same. This understanding began the conversation that eventually led to the science of stress. Bernard pointed out that many body systems need to remain within relatively rigid ranges, or we die: body temperature and the amount of oxygen to the brain are two stand-outs.

McEwen expanded that concept and added his own Greek roots to the lexicon, labeling his additional term 'allostasis,' which emphasizes that systems help keep the body stable by changing themselves. The stress response system is a classic example of a system adapting to a sudden change to keep the body alive when danger lurks: heartbeat, breathing, the amount of glucose in blood, and energy in fat can change swiftly in response to changing circumstances.

Yet McEwen is quick to acknowledge that allostasis is intended to help maintain stability during change and provide energy to cope in circumstances other than life-threatening ones, as well. Your body can adjust to getting up in the morning, a change that stresses body systems, by simply elevating cortisol in the early hours of daybreak, sending extra energy to facilitate the change from prone to upright. If you are not a seasoned public speaker and you are suddenly thrown to the head of a large engagement party to toast your daughter on the eve of her wedding, your body instinctively sends out a squirt of cortisol to give you the boost you need to get through a perceived moment of stress.

Allostasis links the brain, the endocrine system—mainly the adrenal glands—and the immune system to get the energy to the parts of the body that need it the most through a swift and orderly communication system directed by the brain. McEwen developed a framework to explain stress reactions which he calls allostatic load. This expression refers to the state of being stressed out, when damage can result if the allostatic response functions improperly, kicks in inappropriately or does not shut off at the right time. In situations like these, when you cannot calm down after an argument for instance, the system that was designed to protect your body can, instead, tear it down. So often after stressful situations, illness results.

McEwen admonishes that we can also create allostatic load when our

NEUROENDOCRINE STRESS RESPONSE
mediated by the
HYPOTHALAMIC-PITUITARY-ADRENAL (HPA) AXIS

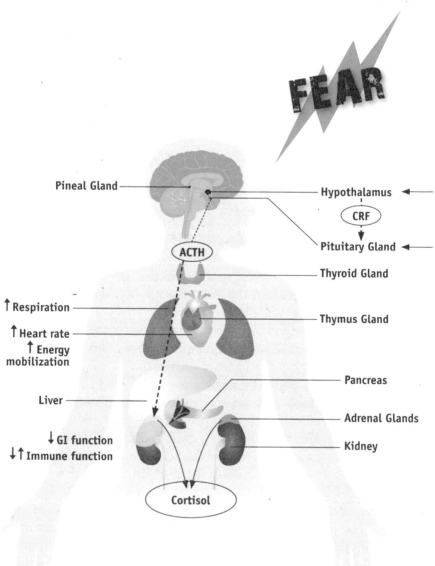

FEAR

Pineal Gland

Hypothalamus

CRF

ACTH

Pituitary Gland

Thyroid Gland

↑Respiration

↑Heart rate

Thymus Gland

↑Energy mobilization

Pancreas

Liver

Adrenal Glands

↓GI function

↓↑Immune function

Kidney

Cortisol

lifestyle causes imbalance: eating too many rich foods puts a metabolic strain on our body; avoiding exercise diminishes the muscles ability to burn glucose; depriving ourselves of enough sleep elevates blood glucose and cortisol which can lead to bone mineral loss; and inherent pessimism bathes us in the dread that can set off the stress response system to our disadvantage.

Cortisol is important as a response to stress, but it also aids your body in returning to the relaxation response and returning to normal. Our stress response system was designed to solve a problem in seconds, not to stay active for hours, days, weeks or even years at a time. While we generally do not live in fear of predators anymore, our daily lives tend to be filled with stressors: frenetic work schedules, overbearing bosses, screaming toddlers, sick family members or financial worries. When stress mode continues over an extended period of time, hormones linger too long. They can cause harm by damaging brain circuitry and disrupting the architecture of the brain—especially in the hippocampus, the area where memory and learning occur. A system designed to protect under threatening situations can actually turn on our body, and destroy brain cells and cause disease when activated too long.

How Does Stress Cause Cardiovascular Disease?

When stressed, our heart pumps faster, driving more blood through our body—responding to the perceived or real stress by pumping more oxygen and glucose. As a result, too much adrenaline stops regulating surges in blood pressure, creating sandpaper-like rough spots on the interior of blood vessels, which turn into scars that allow sticky substances, like cholesterol, to build there and clog the arteries. If one of those scarred blood vessel leads to the heart, the result can be a heart attack; if it leads to an artery in the brain, it can cause a stroke. Inflammation at these rough spots can elevate cholesterol levels and lead many doctors to prescribe statins to reduce cholesterol and stabilize plaque. The cholesterol is merely a marker for the inflammation, so some current thinking suggests we go beyond treating the symptoms and reassess the role of statins and address what is causing the inflammation in the first place. Clearly, folks who live with chronic stress can be more at risk for heart attacks and strokes.

Why Does Stress Have an Adverse Effect on Our Immune System?

Our immune response sends out white blood cells to fight the good fight against pathogens. But over time, when our immune response is activated too long, chronic stress actually kills off these white knights. Current research concludes that stress can ravage parts of the immune system that produce antibodies, reducing your ability to fight infection, even in some cases nudging your immune system into firing on your own body. So under stress over time, you get sick more often, and have a greater risk of developing other autoimmune disorders, such as asthma or diabetes.

What Does Stress Do to Our Brain?

The hippocampus, the seat of memory, responds to stress signals. If you have survived being caught in the thrashes of hurricane winds while stranded on a highway watching the flood waters rise around you and running low on fuel, you will remember the event with colorful details and avoid a late evacuation in the future. Studded with cortisol receptors, the hippocampus, is very responsive to stress signals and, in order to save your life, keeps busy creating the memories of stressful events that can be instantly recalled in future times of crisis.

The hippocampus is also the seat of learning. Stress in the form of perceived fear, can cause cognitive collapse in a classroom, shutting down learning. In a business setting, perceived fear can curtail productivity. Concentration is impaired; performance is diminished; memory is compromised; problem solving is reduced. None of these is a positive harbinger of good report cards for kids or performance reviews for their parents!

Here's what is happening in the brain: Glucocorticoids are the villains. These hormones are also secreted by the adrenal glands. In excessive doses over time, they can scramble neural networks, many of which might be storing your favorite memories. They can even prevent the hippocampus from producing new neurons, in some cases going so far as to kill hippocampal cells themselves. Nasty!

But there is hope. Exercise produces the magical BDNF—Brain Derived Neurotrophic Factor, a protein known as a neurotrophin. Medina describes it as the Miracle-Gro® that keeps neurons alive and growing in the midst of the battle going on in the hippocampus. But this fertilizer cannot withstand an interminable siege by glucocorticoids. With too strong an attack, glucocorticoids can turn off the gene that makes the BDNF, disabling the natural defense normally available to the hippocampus. Forgetfulness, depression, and diminished reasoning can result from this deregulation of thought processes. As Medina concludes, stress hurts learning; stress hurts people.

Buffers to Stress

In young children, the brain can get back to its baseline through interaction in a protective relationship with a supportive adult. The National Council on the Developing Child confirms that genetics and early life experiences set the stress thermostat level. If elevated too much in early years, it takes less to trigger the stress system as an adult. Over time, stress can inhibit your child's immune system and then lead to health issues in later life. Teens endure unprecedented stressors in the current climate of achievement mania that surrounds them. We will unpack that culprit in Chapter Nine.

Teaching our teens healthy stress-management techniques is essential. It starts with practicing what we preach. Preserving our health is within our grasp if we manage our stress loads better and reflect on our lifestyles. Whether or not stress damages us is a consequence of the interaction between the world we choose to live in and our physiological capacity to manage it.

Certainly, stressors that threaten the control we have over our lives are on the rise: the information explosion makes it harder to manage the data that floods our everyday lives; media can bring in violence and perpetuate distance from our friends; technology breeds a sedentary existence; geographic isolation of family members robs us of the support systems that can support us in trying times.

How do you know when your stress level has moved from positive to tolerable or even toxic? Some indicators that the light is blinking, that allostatic load is eroding your quality of life are: irritability, impatience, anxiousness at work, feeling in high demand with little validation, too little time for personal activities, not feeling fully engaged with family when you're finally with them, rarely expressing appreciation, reacting to demands rather than responding or reflecting, working into the evenings, not having an email-free weekend or vacation, and difficulty focusing. We humans like to go beyond our natural capabilities. We extend our cognitive reach by using drugs—caffeine, nicotine, sugar—to extend our capacity to focus over longer, often unnatural, periods of time.

We take our capacity for granted. We expect ourselves to mimic our electronic devices: run continuously at high speeds for long periods of time. If we manage our time, we will finish the product. But what about when demand exceeds capacity?

Balancing the conflicting demands of this century for ourselves and our children, in our workplaces and in our homes, requires enormous reserves of physical and emotional energy. We plug our iPhones and iPads into an electric circuit to recharge them. But refueling our tank requires us to make strategic choices. We have to cut through the frenetic pace and the abundant demands that deplete our reserves and leave us breathless.

For us, as adults, living under constant stress means we are unable to connect to our children at the end of the day. For our teenagers, it means they cannot benefit from the majority of what they are trying so hard to learn. More importantly, their brain development can be hindered.

As a species, we seek balance. Homeostasis keeps us alive. Allostasis, when our internal systems shift themselves to achieve that balance, is a constant pattern of protection versus damage. Studies remind us that our lifestyle can tilt the hypothalamic-pituitary-adrenal (HPA) axis and increase our cortisol levels even when we are not anxious about something. Perhaps as ravaging as the elevated cortisol on our biology are the coping techniques we tend to use to offset the perceived stressors: doughnuts, cokes, coffee, pulling all nighters at the office—piling on yet another layer of stress to whatever caused the stress in the first place.

What is the story you tell yourself about why you continue with the corrosive habits that systematically undermine the impact of your energy? Does your teenager tell the same story? What can you do when demand exceeds capacity to restore balance in your life, so that you are able to create the environment and build the relationships your children need to build genetic flourish? *This is temporary. This is what it takes. Don't know how to change.* What is the underlying behavior that keeps you from living the behaviors that would make you healthier, happier and more productive? What is the perceived guilt that might be sapping your energy; how can you overcome it?

Acknowledging these destructive behaviors is the beginning of fixing them for yourself, modeling them for your teen and working toward healthy homeostasis in your life.

My grandmother said it, and McEwen's research confirms it: we all need balance. Teens need it as much as young children and as much as we do. That means reducing stress. We can start by questioning our activities to prioritize: is what I have signed up for good for my family, my career or a cause I care about? We can't control the world around us, but we can commit to more sleep, regular exercise, healthier diets, consistent socialization, and a life that has meaning and purpose. New habits that that are body and brain healthy can be a catalyst to the ravages of stress. Let's take a look at our sleep habits. Getting adequate rest is the easiest way to make improvements in brain of all ages, and America is not getting to bed on time!

Neuro-Parenting Principles
CHAPTER FIVE

1. Stress happens when we feel out of control.
2. Prolonged stress can kill brain cells and compromise health.
3. Lifestyles can impose stress on our bodies.
4. We can buffer stress with careful planning and shifting our priorities.

THE
HIDDEN
COST OF SLEEP
DEBT

f healthy thirty-year-olds are sleep-deprived for six days—averaging four hours of sleep per night—parts of their body chemistry soon revert to that of a sixty-year-old. It would take a week to get back to their thirty-year-old system. Sleep deprivation activates the stress response system. So thirty-turning-sixty can happen when you subject your body to prolonged periods of real or perceived stress, whether by bathing yourself in dread and pessimism as we have just discussed in Chapter Five or by not getting enough sleep, as you will see in the following pages.

Sleep Deprivation

We know from personal experience and from the literature on sleep research that the brain starts to malfunction with sleep deprivation. An A student who gets under seven hours of sleep on week nights can drop from the top 10 percent to the bottom 9 percent in academic performance. Seniors in high school average only slightly more than six and a half hours of sleep a night—many are sleeping hardly more than four hours on a regular basis. According to Mary Carskadon at Brown University, teens need nine and a quarter hours of sleep per night for healthy brain development and cognitive flexibility.

Cumulative sleep losses during the week result in cumulative deficits—and the sleep debt can carry over into future weeks with a compounding effect over time. A study looking at soldiers noted a 30-percent drop in cognitive skill, resulting in a drop in efficiency in operating complex military equipment with the loss of a full night's sleep, and a 60-percent drop following the loss of two nights of sleep.

Not Just Sleepy: Fat, Old, and Crabby

New studies reveal that sleep deprivation hinders the body's ability to utilize food by 30 percent. The ability to make insulin and extract energy from glucose begins to fail. Simultaneously, cravings for food increase because the body's stress hormone levels rise. If you are gaining weight, consider closing your computer or putting down your iPad and climbing into bed!

Sleep affects metabolism. Sleep loss elevates cortisol. Tired people have trouble inhibiting behavior because their impulse control diminishes. Tired brains perseverate—a fancy term for obsessing—often on the wrong answer. Sleep deprivation hits the hippocampus more than the amygdala. Sleep-deprived people recall gloomy memories more than pleasant ones. Sleep loss inhibits thinking, reducing you to reacting rather than reflecting, and it affects judgment, memory, mood, and dexterity. Wow. Let's take a nap before we go any further with this!

How Many Bricks Are Weighing Down Your Mental Backpack?

Go for a minute with current research that says you need eight hours of sleep each night. Look at the multiples. One brick for one hour of sleep. Lose two hours of sleep, add two bricks to your mental backpack. Get an extra hour of sleep past the eight hours, take a brick out. See where you are at the end of a week:

Monday: productive, busy day—7 hours of sleep. Add a brick.

Tuesday: more tasks to complete—6 hours of sleep. Add 2 bricks.

Wednesday: big assignment due on Friday—5 hours of sleep. Add 3 bricks.

Thursday: all due tomorrow—4 hours of sleep. Add 4 bricks.

Friday: the extra weight is curtailing productivity, 10 bricks constitute a heavy burden!

With a heavy sleep debt, shut-eye over the weekend needs to make up the extra ten hours of sleep over and above the requisite daily eight hours. Sleep debts can build over weeks, months and years, taking a toll on your health, relationships, productivity, and attitude.

What Happens During Sleep

Sleep and stress are closely related. Irregular sleep patterns—staying up late to finish a project, catch a good movie or pull an all-nighter before a test—can tip the stress response systems against teens (and us) by elevating cortisol levels. Our Circadian, or daily, rhythm, is tied to the natural flow of our stress hormones in helping us adapt to change. When this system gets out of sync due to sleep deprivation over a prolonged period, our health can be at risk and our productivity can be compromised. Sleep deprivation is a mood changer and can diminish our ability to cope effectively with everyday challenges. Doctors also now look for changes in sleep patterns in cases of depression.

Remember that our brain is built for survival and that sensory input triggers calculated responses. Sleep must be very important, because the sleep state shuts down our very important visual sensory input, in particular, and renders us vulnerable to our enemies. In fact, all muscle activity ceases except that needed for breathing during certain intervals of our sleep cycle.

Yet our brain does not actually stop working and rest when we go to sleep. In fact, when we look at the rhythmical activity in predictable sleep cycles, we see that the night shift comes in and squads of neurons crackle electrical commands across the system, appearing to some as though the brain might, in fact, be working even harder during sleep. The only time the brain is less active during sleep than awake is during the deepest part of non-REM sleep, which comprises only about 20 percent of the sleep cycle.

So how does sleep become restorative if the brain is working so diligently? Other parts of the body do rest, even if the brain is fast at work.

Bad Things Happen to Bodies That Do Not Get Enough Sleep

When your teen doesn't get a good night's sleep, it's not "no big deal." Thinking and decision-making are impaired; cognitive flexibility declines rapidly in direct proportion to sleep deprivation. Three hours of missed sleep can have the same adverse effect as four glasses of wine. Four hours of missed sleep is categorically the same as driving drunk. Would you let your teen go to school drunk? No. So why do we place demands on our high-school children that cause them to lose so much sleep? From a learning point of view, they might as well be drunk.

William Dement, the father of sleep studies, says that brains, like soldiers on a battlefield, are actually locked in vicious, biological combat, where legions of brain cells and biochemicals clash over different agendas. Dement describes these opposing forces as fighting during the day and night, alternating cycles, alternating victory and defeat, neither force ever a victor, but together generating the wake-sleep cycles that happen every day, every night.

Science notes that our body's internal alarm clock, the Circadian rhythm that signals us by bringing on the yawns when our body is beginning to short-circuit, is housed deep in the hypothalamus. One army, the Circadian arousal system, does its best to keep you awake, while the opposing army, the homeostatic sleep drive, wants to usher you off to bed to sleep, to dream, to keep you there with all the might of its neurons, hormones, and chemicals.

The exact amount of sleep needed and the schedule for acquiring it varies with individuals and their stage of development. The question for teenagers is whether they are getting as much as they need or whether they are acquiring a sleep debt that can, ultimately, damage their brain, their health, and their performance. And the same questions hold for all of us.

How Does Light Affect Sleep?

I am rethinking the presence of night-lights in my grandchildren's bedrooms. I used to think they were comforting—and innocuous—until I learned darkness permits the pineal gland to produce melatonin, while light inhibits its production.

Think about all the digital devices that blink in the night in the modern bedroom and interrupt our sleep cycles—the green dot on our phone charger, red dot on our house alarm, bright dot on our iHome and blue dot on our plasma screen that signals a connection to its mother ship in the interstices of our laundry room closet. Even blackout curtains might not give us the darkness we need to generate the chemical messengers in our body for a good night's sleep if we juice up our digital extensions of ourselves in the same room where we are sleeping.

Melatonin is a crucial part of the system that regulates the sleep-wake cycle by chemically causing drowsiness and lowering body temperature. Secretion of melatonin, as well as its level in the bloodstream, peaks in the middle of the night and gradually falls off during the second half of the night. If you choose, you can have a sonic-boom alarm clock wake you up by shaking your mattress while emitting intergalactic sounds and flashing blue lights! This digital delight can certainly start your day with shock and awe—try to get back to homeostasis after that surge of cortisol.

Teen Sleep Cycles Command Attention

Mary Carskadon does research on teen sleep patterns in her labs at Brown University. She reveals that during the teen years the nightly schedule of melatonin release is delayed, leading to later sleeping and waking times for teens. The bold high schools that have recognized this developmental change in sleep cycles and have implemented later start times for their teens, have witnessed an astonishing rise in student grades and safety. Automobile associations and insurance statistics confirm that more teens are in automobile wrecks in the early hours going to school than at any other time of day—even more than on weekend nights, when most would assume the dangers of automobile collisions would be the highest.

School schedules and programs are often made more for the convenience of adults than for the benefit of children. In general, those schedules force teens into a variant of jetlag every day, generating detentions for being tardy while forgetting that teens simply cannot wake up as easily as they could before high school. Policy makers and administrators take heed: we should not try to beat out Mother Nature.

In addition to its function as the synchronizer of our biological clock, melatonin can exert powerful antioxidant activity in our body. In animal models, melatonin has demonstrated its ability to prevent the damage to DNA by some carcinogens, in some cases curtailing the mechanisms that can cause some cancers and neurodegenerative diseases. Interrupting sleep interrupts melatonin production. Bad things happen to your body when you do not get enough sleep.

Sleep Is An Important Part of the Learning Process

Listening to the chatter of neurons as they process information in a study of rats in mazes suggests that maybe learning occurs during sleep by replaying the events of the day. The rats seemed to consolidate the day's learning. Humans also seem to organize and consolidate the events of the day during different phases of the sleep cycle. Science is suggesting that perhaps sleep is a necessary part of the learning process.

Sleep Cycles

Sleep involves the interplay of brain circuits that move through different cycles. Brain waves slow down in a progressive manner, while muscles begin to relax. During REM (rapid eye movement) sleep, only the muscles for breathing stay active. Cycles of slow wave sleep and REM sleep alternate.

With sleep loss, the body loses its ability to extract glucose from the bloodstream. The prefrontal cortex suffers from the loss of this stream of basic energy. Executive function diminishes. Tired people experience cognitive challenges and are often accident prone. Neurons lose plasticity with fatigue and are less capable of forming the synaptic connections necessary to encode memory.

While sleeping, the brain stores what it has learned during the day. New information is synthesized by the hippocampus in Stage I sleep, and certain genes up-regulate. Sleep deprivation adversely affects the hippocampus and your metabolism. Sleep loss elevates cortisol.

Sleep Disorders

Sleep disorders affect up to seventy million people, and most remain undiagnosed and untreated. Sleeping and breathing go together. Many folks have respiratory problems that can lead to sleep apnea, in which a person regularly stops breathing, a condition that can lead to serious health problems. Children who are sleep deprived can manifest behavioral and learning problems. Many children diagnosed with ADHD actually have sleep apnea. Forty-percent of children who snore will suffer from sleep deprivation and experience daytime sleepiness, leading to poor performance and a gloomier outlook. Being cognizant of a young child's sleep pattern will often provide clues to a child's disposition. Monitor your own sleep pattern as well as your child's. Good sleep helps build the good relationships that can mitigate the barriers to healthy brain development. Responsive relationships are crucial to children. We'll explore why in Chapter Seven.

Neuro-Parenting Principles
CHAPTER SIX

1. Sleep affects health; sleep affects metabolism.
2. Light can interrupt sleep cycles, preventing a restorative night's sleep.
3. Sleep disorders affect over seventy million people.
4. Children can experience sleep disorders that can impact their behavior.

BE
HERE
NOW

The Best Gift We Can Give Someone Is Our Full Attention

How many times have you started a conversation with your teen, your spouse or a close friend and quickly found their eyes diverted to their iPhone or Blackberry to check messages or, worse, respond to one as you continued speaking. Did you feel a little irritated, a little neglected for an instant? Eye contact feeds your brain the information it needs to gauge an appropriate response; it interprets the body language that accompanies the words, sleuthing out the nuance in the message. Remember, your brain cannot multi-task. Your brain uses passive selective attention, switching from one signal to another. You have shifted from a "serve-and-return" conversation to a soliloquy. The connection between you has been momentarily broken.

Your child feels the same way when he asks you a question, and you do not look up from your computer or iPhone to respond. You get two chances, then he moves on. You have communicated by your lack of engagement that your child and his message are not very important to you. You have missed the moment for engagement.

My colleague told me with amusement that he negotiated a deal to his advantage because he was the only one in the boardroom not on his digital device, catching an email or dashing off a quick text here and there—he was giving his full attention to the terms while the others were flipping in and out of the conversation, missing details. Your brain cannot multi-task. Hear it now. Believe it. It is true. Passive selective attention can compromise a deal—or an important relationship.

Early Development Occurs Through Relationships

Leaving our son's home, we looked back and saw little Grace scrambling up on to the chair, then banging on the window while waving both hello and goodbye. We smiled and returned our grandchild's wave, touched by her bright eyes and expectant gaze—simple love and connectedness.

We see explorer babies—crawling and climbing, touching and tasting— trying to make sense of their worlds, trying to figure out their place among the people and the objects that surround them. They are changing and growing their brains at every turn. The first place they learn is at home—their first environment. The relationships formed there will be the ones that shape how children feel about themselves and the people who comprise their world. This sense of exploration doesn't stop as children enter adolescence. We need to foster it, and the best way to do that is by giving them our full attention, show them we are listening when they ask us a question or pause to share a significant moment.

Young children develop in the context of relationships, which, in turn, shape their brain development. A child's initial emotional security stems from how he perceives the people around him: can he count on them for protection and support? A child is constantly initiating a signal and responding to a caregiver, generally his mother, to see if he has a reliable baseline from which to explore safely. Going back to our image of the Brain Open, it's interesting to note that Dr. Jack Shonkoff, Director of the Center on the Developing Child, points to this "serve-and-return" dialogue as the basis of a growth relationship for a child. These responsive relationships start early and form the foundation for healthy brain development.

Attachment Styles Affect Development

As parents, we're responsible for the safety of our progeny. Attachment is the scientific term for trust that an infant develops with the parent or primary caregiver, who responds to the child's distress. A relationship between the child and parent develops based on the response style of this primary caregiver, usually the mother. The quality of this attachment lays the foundation for emotional development and can shape a child's entire life. John Bowlby proposed the first ideas about Attachment Theory when he espoused that infants figure out ways to get the attention of their caregivers as a means of survival, beginning with crying.

Later, a baby uses additional signals to keep the caregiver close: smiling, vocalizing, crawling, and eventually walking. A tired or fearful baby will send out more signals to pull in the support needed to return to a state of contentment and safety, moving closer to the reassurance provided from the mother's physical presence. As the attachment relationship grows, an emotional bond begins to develop; in addition, a pattern of interaction begins to form between the two participants. With adequate contact and proximity, the infant can count on the mother for safety and can begin exploration. Here starts the differentiation between secure and insecure attachment.

Secure vs. Insecure Attachment

Building on Bowlby's theories, Mary Ainsworth, a developmental psychologist known for her work on Attachment Theory, used observations of mother and child reunions to produce empirical data that substantiated the significant differences between secure and insecure attachment on cognitive and emotional development. Ainsworth found that mothers who were less responsive to their baby's needs had babies who were less secure. She evolved three primary patterns of attachment: secure, avoidant, and dependent. Secure, or positive, attachment can lead to healthy emotional growth. Insecure, or poor, attachment can put adult relationships at risk and perpetuate dysfunctional family cycles across generations. What are the differences?

Secure children know that they can count on their mothers in moments of distress, that she will be responsive, and that they will feel better soon.

Avoidant children have figured out that they cannot count on their mothers, so these youngsters will not even trouble themselves to seek comfort from their mothers when in distress.

Dependent children are not certain what to think about their mothers, who are sometimes unavailable and unreliable. They see their mothers as having their own agendas. Dependent children will approach their mothers, but not with confidence.

As language develops, so does the ability to deal with emotion, using language as a mediator. As research about secure and faulty attachment evolves, the idea that understanding emotion may have an impact on relationships has emerged. Families that offer their children emotional scaffolding—giving them language to understand and articulate their emotions—empower their children to navigate adult relationships with more success. When we are there for our children—and they trust that we are fully present—they are able to explore their world, learn, and connect with greater confidence and success.

The Zone of Proximal Development

Social interaction has a fundamental role in the development of cognition. In the early part of the twentieth century, Lev Vygotsky conducted significant research and developed theory in cognitive development that laid the foundational beliefs in this area for several decades. He espoused that innate abilities develop over time through social interaction and the use of tools to move a child toward functioning at his or her fullest potential. Vygotsky's concept of the Zone of Proximal Development refers to the gap between the level at which a child can function at a task independently and the level to which a child can be nudged with scaffolding from an adult or a more competent peer to perform at an even higher level, manifesting potential for development. What does that mean? There is a difference between what a child can achieve with and without support.

Our grandson Walker enjoys doing jigsaw puzzles. My husband and I went to his house one evening for dinner and brought him a new puzzle. If we put the puzzle on the table and went into the kitchen to visit with his parents, he would have moved around the pieces and gotten frustrated. Instead, we suggested he look at edges and corners, helping him identify ways to match patterns, all the while encouraging him to try. We gave him tools. The combination of instruction and support escalated his performance and success. The zone of learning is where social interaction and support move him forward. Then, later, he can work a jigsaw puzzle on his own, because he has internalized the tools and does not need the encouragement to proceed on his own to a successful conclusion.

Vygotsky found his concept of the Zone of Proximal Development particularly meaningful because it expressed the significance of social interaction on learning. Current research in neuroscience suggests that neural networks, which build through experience and exposure, tend to confirm Vygotsky's brilliance. These scientific explanations support Vygotsky's creative thinking about how humans parse together information into a meaningful whole through social interaction. These concepts seem reasonable for continued learning through the adult years.

Vygotsky believed experience and enrichment trigger innate genetic predisposition. What does that mean? We learn from experience. In the beginning, we obtain meaningful tools—like words—as a reflexive response. We move into self-modulation, or impulse control. We begin using our tools as external devices, directing others and performing productive tasks; then, ultimately, we transition into internalized speech. This self-talk becomes thinking, the tool by which a developing child manages himself and his world. As children generate these tools they are constantly testing them on the world around them. We've all seen the reaction when a young child utters a particularly foul word at a family party or the pride that the family takes when that same youngster says "please" and "thank you." This process, known as cultural mediation, keeps motivation high and learning astute.

Project that concept into the teenage years, and it tends to look more like this: A teen expresses a creative idea in class; the teacher responds with cynicism and embarrasses him. Cognitive collapse occurs. Learning happens in trust relationships, and the quality of the relationship affects the quality of the learning. Let's look at some of the implications of this dynamic.

Relationships as Predictors of Quality of Life

We've established that children grow up in relationships, the quality of which will become predictors of future productivity, health, and quality of life. Urie Bronfenbrenner, the Cornell University child development scholar who developed this groundbreaking Ecological Systems Theory, warned that the hectic pace of modern life poses a serious threat to our children. Bronfenbrenner cautioned that we now know what it takes to enable families to work the magic that only they can perform. He was quick to ask if families were willing to make the sacrifices and the investment necessary.

Who's Minding the Children?

When your children were younger, you might have used a daycare facility because professional responsibilities took you out of your home. Or perhaps an early learning center marketed the edge it would give your child on future competition. You may have employed a nanny, live-in or otherwise, to give yourself some time away, to allow you to continue community and social pursuits. Surrogate care-givers can help families to function more smoothly and with less stress, but we need to treat them as if we are playing with fire.

Regardless of the circumstances, in order for healthy development, children must have that serve-and-return relationship with a consistent caregiver who is an active listener and who engages in, as the National Scientific Council on the Developing Child describes so beautifully, *the duet of smiles, gestures, and animated vocalizations that builds the brain and nurtures abilities.*

For over a hundred years, science has demonstrated what we've always known in our hearts: children need caring, conscientious, connected adults to help them reach their full potential. So what's going on in our country today? Why do we as a group seem to be ignoring this common-sense, traditional, and scientifically supported concept? Why do we not define the role of caretakers more carefully and make sure they are adequately prepared to offer our children the kind of responsiveness they need? Let's look at who's really minding the children.

Across demographic lines, childcare workers are often the lowest paid and the least educated. Their jobs have the highest turnover. Many parents have no option but to leave their children in facilities that cannot provide proper nurturing. Maternity leave in the United States is one of the least appropriate for positive child development in the industrialized world. Federal law states that new mothers can have six weeks off—with or without pay, depending on company policy—with an option of an additional six weeks off without pay. They are guaranteed they can return to a job at the same level, but not necessarily the same post. To receive this leave, they must file for temporary disability. Disability? As a mother and a grandmother, I find this a poor choice of words. As an educator, I find it inaccurate.

Schools—institutions centered on the education and development of children—exercise this policy with their faculties and staff as well. Women are incentivized to get back into the work force quickly after giving birth, either to maintain a hard-earned position in industry or because they cannot afford the loss of pay. As women spend less time in extended families, they spend less time becoming familiar with the techniques of caring for babies. Many first-time mothers doubt their abilities and knowledge, and turn their newborns over to a baby nurse, relinquishing those early moments so important for the bonding that builds secure attachment.

Remember the classic children's book, *Are You My Mother?* A little bird hatches in the nest as his mother has gone out to find him a worm. He hops from nest to nest looking for her. He finds other animals and asks each one, "Are you my mother?" Eventually, he lands himself at the brink of danger. If all the primary caregivers are out looking for worms, what will the little birds do?

The Cost of Ignoring the Research

The future health of our children, our families, our economy, our culture depends on our willingness to be active partners—leaders—in our children's miraculous developmental process. As individuals, are we willing to sacrifice the time? As a society, are we willing to make the investment in areas like maternity leave and paternity leave? Are we willing to value the people who work in the childcare and early education industry so they can be prepared to provide our children with proper care? Savvy policy makers who stay close to cutting-edge research will know that it takes a lot more than just babysitting to keep a child safe. When we understand what is going on in the brain in the first five years of life, we cannot entrust our little ones to inferior relationships. When we rationalize that we can't afford these approaches, what we overlook is that the capital we are using to support our prosperity is our children's future. Building meaningful early relationships is imperative for building the neural connections critical for healthy brain development.

The strongest early relationships continue to be with parents for most young children. While the need for these relationships continues into adolescence, the role of the parent changes. Teens turn to friends, appropriately so. Anticipating this upcoming shift, savvy parents of pre-teens can begin to think about where they can nurture potential relationships with mentors who will take a personal interest in their children as their teens look to form a broader network. Remember the impact of internships we discussed in Chapter Three? The power of those experiences came in large part from a relationship with a mentor. These mentors can be found among family friends, business associates, scoutmasters, church leaders, teachers or local community organizations. At this point, parents should start thinking about internships or special projects as a means to build relationships that can also seed a passion or unpack a personal interest. Parents need to remain active listeners and attentive, but understand that their role will be different for a while as their teens reach outside their comfort zones.

One inherent casualty of applying the *use it or lose it* lesson and getting anxious about the college application process ahead can be a Tiger Mom's interpretation that these upcoming drivers mean a child should be enrolled in every sports/art/enrichment program available. It is an easy mistake to make. Parents can rationalize that undue immersion will make teens blinking geniuses—or, in some cases, buy some extra time at the office or leave room for a high-powered social life. Be vigilant. Watch for the flashing lights signaling that your teen has had enough. It's never too late to make better choices. And these choices can make significant, quantifiable differences in our children's development throughout adolescence and beyond. When we understand the implications of the research, we can create healthier environments for our children. Knowledge can empower us with the courage to say 'no' to many of the pressures of modern life that can compromise our teens' development.

Let's look more closely at how Bronfenbrenner defined family and community and the significant roles people play in a child's life.

Ecological Systems Theory

There are multiple influences that impact developing children and their parents. The Ecological Systems Theory, proposed by Urie Bronfenbrenner, describes five environmental systems within a culture that influence a child's development.

Microsystem: comprised of family members in closest relationship with a child.

Mesosystem: connects the child to school and community experiences.

Exosystem: highlights the social systems that influence a child but do not include him—like a parent's workplace whose policies, such as flexible work hours, could have an indirect impact on a child's development if a parent is unable to be available to meet a child's needs in a moment of personal crisis.

Macrosystem: reflects cultural attitudes that will filter down to a child, such as laws and religious beliefs.

Chronosystem: references disruptive events that can impact development at sensitive periods in a child's life—divorce, illness, a natural disaster—and might alter a child's life and compromise the ability to nurture resilience.

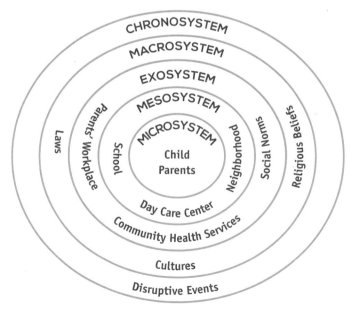

Bronfenbrenner's theory revealed that interpersonal relationships, beginning with parent-child, did not exist in a vacuum. They are embedded in the larger social structures of community, society, economics, and politics. Current neuroscience research substantiates that the brain does everything in context, and confirms these earlier discoveries about the impact of an environment of relationships on genetic expression and flourish. While his answers are not easy and demand responsibility and action, Bronfenbrenner has been credited with changing America's approach to child rearing and creating a new, interdisciplinary scholarly field. Now if we can just get these ideas out into the mainstream, we can all support each other in being present for our children. The time they spend in our homes is only a fraction of our expected lifespan. Surely we can prioritize being present and responsive during this time.

Crazy about You!

Think about the adults in your life as you were growing up. Your relationship was different with each of them. Who was your champion? Who seemed to get you? Who believed you were particularly gifted in a certain area? Did that person have an impact on who you are today? You're probably nodding your head. Most of us are lucky enough to have had significant adults in our life who saw our potential, articulated it to us and did not allow us to give up on it. Research supports the impact these relationships have on us.

The renowned developmental pediatrician T. Berry Brazelton confirms emphatically that children thrive in an environment where relationships are based on unconditional love and meaningful engagement with a consistent caregiver. Bronfenbrenner puts it simply: every child deserves to have somebody who is absolutely crazy about him.

When our children were young, they were fresh-faced and full of wonder. They presented us with the flowers, bugs, and rocks they found in their explorations with the trust that we would respond with attention and delight. Though they are taller now and can sometimes be off-putting with their peer-driven behavior and their emotional swings, they are still those developing minds, full of wonder. Now more than ever, we need to be there for them—just a little less visible—scaffolding, supporting, listening, and guiding them as their exploration of life takes them to higher and sometimes more dizzying altitudes.

Neuro-Parenting Principles
CHAPTER SEVEN

1. Active listening and eye contact suggest that someone is important to you.

2. Early relationships lay the foundation for healthy brain development.

3. Children learn best in their zone of proximal development.

4. Childcare workers are often the lowest paid and least equipped to work with children.

5. Consistent and attentive caregivers are important for healthy brain development.

6. Children learn in a series of relationships: family, school, community, world.

7. Children need someone who cares enormously about them and feels they are special.

MEDIA:
MANAGING ITS
POTENTIAL

We've accepted the notion for years now that alert parents can develop family patterns that build meaningful relationships through active engagement. It begins with healthy lifestyle choices during the prenatal period and after birth moves to activities like reading to their children daily to create personal connections that will get even stronger over the years ahead. We know what to expect when we're expecting; we know too much sugar is bad for our kids, and we know reading is good for them. We sense that digital media is bad for them, but is it a fear of the new—and a reasonable reaction—or a misguided notion? Before we look at the impact of media on teens and how we can best guide that dynamic, let's examine what science has known and is discovering about the effects of media in various formats on cognitive development.

What Is It About Reading That Is so Good for Kids?

How I look forward to snuggling up with my grandsons Prescott and Watt while taking a journey together through a new or old favorite book; our *Never Tease a Weasel* is worn on the edges with a few pages now loose from its many readings over the years. The Jim Trelease *Read Aloud Handbook* sits in a place of honor on our family's bookshelf.

Reading is not just about vocabulary enrichment; it builds meaningful relationships, which can nurture the positive mindsets that are predictors for personal resilience. Reading fosters brain development and scaffolds resilience, while mediating external factors that can interrupt healthy growth. Reading stimulates the engagement so critical for gene expression to flourish. *Curious George* gets in and out of trouble; *George and Martha* show us vicariously the value of growing friendships; and *Lilly's Purple Plastic Purse* is simply fun to read out loud. These classic stories can become great conversation starters with our young children.

Children's literature is rich with captivating characters, creative art forms, vivid imagination, compelling stories, and figurative language. Reading to children is replete with opportunities to share joy, explain sadness, and give root to the adventure of learning about a child's emerging world. Each genre can be used in multiple ways to match the individual differences among young children. Stories can be read, told, discussed, or even created along the way, as the reader would choose. Children can change the endings to meet their own needs and expectations. The world of reading is an invitation to make new friends in the characters and explore new ideas in the messages.

Multiple ways of presenting stories, expressing their themes and lessons, and multiple ways of connecting emotionally with the plots and characters enrich each family's experience as they discover together the adventures ahead. Reading is an excellent vehicle for engagement, an excellent catalyst for building resilience vicariously through the story lines. All this should only be enhanced when reading is augmented with images and animation, right?

I'm not going to answer that yet. Stay with me on the benefits of reading a little longer. It will put the impact of modern media on teens' digital brains into more meaningful context. Let's look at a few key benefits of reading, including building resiliency and language development.

Reading Builds Resiliency

A young child needs an environment that provides warmth, continuity, and security—all characteristic of a meaningful reading relationship between a sensitive parent and an inquisitive child, all predictors of later resiliency. Early exposure to engagement with books—not early reading, but early exposure to age-appropriate readiness tasks—can build the intellectual curiosity necessary for later academic success, another foundation for building resiliency. Parents can give their children a personal edge, help honor individual differences in development and scaffold the growth and resiliency that they seek. Helping children flourish by developing their natural potential will give children the foundation they need for becoming healthy, productive adults with the ability to adapt to a changing world.

Reading Supports Language Development

Empirical data from Maryanne Wolf, director of the Center for Reading and Language Research at Tufts University, confirms the patterns of language development in children: from sounds, to words, to sentences, to stories. Oral language turns into written language. Children experience enormous growth in language starting at about eighteen months, reflective of a caregiver's vocabulary and engagement. Reading can scaffold the language development and positive attitude that parents seek to build in their children.

Books can introduce language, art, and ideas: from concrete to abstract, from Silverstein to Shakespeare. Children will be facing a changing world, one that will reward those who can think creatively and adapt quickly. Reading can be a catalyst for guiding a child through personal experience, helping to organize life events, and building a positive mindset for a productive life.

Early verbal scores are predictors of higher achievement scores later. Betty Hart and Todd Risely, whose pioneering research examined child-parent talk in families, have rich data that manifests how vocabulary gaps among children who start pre-school continue throughout early education. In your teen's life, reading is a better preparation for standardized testing than any expensive, short-term preparation course. Just like money accruing interest for retirement, the return-on-investment is by far more predictable and deep when the preparation starts in infancy, in a reading environment at home. We've all seen the ads from the investment houses: we can help you reach your retirement goals, no matter how well you've been able to save in the past. It's never too late to reap benefit from reading.

Just because our kids don't want us to read to them at bedtime anymore doesn't mean our habits regarding reading don't affect them. When our teens are at a developmental stage where peers impact them proportionally more than at earlier stages, we cannot bombard them with lectures or even extol the benefits and joys of reading. Parents must model what they value. We can learn from the master: Ronald McDonald. Advertise what you want your kids to buy. Be a reader. Let your children see you with a book in your hand, a predetermined stack by your bedside, on your desk or by your computer. Choose your books the way you choose your friends: with hours to live, not hours to kill. Parents who are readers will have children who are readers. It is that simple. Hold on to this understanding of the deep and positive value of reading on cognitive and social development as we fast-forward into an exploration of the media options and pressures teens face today.

Digital Brains: Growing Up with Media

Even with the many hours I spend with teenagers each week and the ongoing education I have had, I am still the product of an earlier generation. I grew up with dial telephones and black-and-white television that went off the air after the news. The miraculous screen of the Etch-a-Sketch was considered cutting-edge when I was in college. As I was attempting to mask my frustration with my new iPad, my six-year-old grandchild, Paysan, edged over to me. She soothed my angst and gently explained, "Just slide your finger across the screen like this. You can do it, Grammy. I will help you." Scaffolding, at all ages, moves learning forward.

Electronic tablets, Wi-Fi, e-books, e-readers, iPhones, built-in navigation devices, all these wonders of technology and information transmission are just part of the landscape to my grandchildren. They grew up here. While I find this digital world to be a fascinating and exciting country, I am not fluent in the language and will never be as fluent as they will; I will probably always need a dictionary. They are digital natives; I am a digital immigrant with an accent!

In Chapter Four, we looked at how the brain constantly adapts itself based on experience. What does the digital experience mean? Does the transmission of information through electronic media have the same positive impact on children as reading does? Is it better? Does a high level of immersion in media impact teens positively or negatively? The Kaiser studies indicate that the average American teen has eight-and-a-half hours of screen time each day. With what we know about the nature of the brain, it is folly to imagine that all this screen time is not rewiring brains across the country. The question is how? And what should we do about it?

As the technology industry generates one miraculous product after another, research must scramble to provide empirical data about the impact of digital media on the brain. Luckily, brain science is progressing in a quick two-step with technology, and information sharing exponentially impacts the abilities of researchers. We may be immigrants in this digital world, but we are determined to succeed and make this new land safe and prosperous for future generations. Let's look at the current landscape of digital media.

Electronic Books

E-books have found their way into backpacks and briefcases, into boardrooms and now classrooms. Logically so. They are portable; you can read them in dark corners, on airplanes and in bedrooms without a flashlight. I catch a glimpse of freshmen in Harvard Yard reading their e-books, which glow in the dark like fireflies, as I dash across the yard to help teach my evening class. You can now go beyond carrying two books to carrying seventy-five books with you if you choose to download with diligence. What can digital books do for learning?

David Rose, a developmental neuropsychologist who develops new technologies for learning, founded the Center for Applied Special Technology (CAST), where he has developed his framework known as Universal Design for Learning (UDL). Rose lectures at Harvard and encourages folks to think about "print disability" rather than "child disability," when the print fails to engage a child who might be struggling to become a fluent reader. Publishers are now required to provide digital source files for textbooks. How refreshing: the print has the disability, not the child.

With digital books, you can manipulate the text to scaffold the child at his point of need and get him into his zone of proximal development. You can change the font size or color, add links for definitions or translation from a foreign language, connect to sources with maps or historical references or artwork to add meaning to the printed text. If you went to work out, and the person who used the equipment before you was taller and heavier, you would need to adjust the machine to your body type and size. Digital books in classrooms can be adjusted to the child. Differentiated instruction and individualized learning can begin here.

Research confirms that emotion drives learning. When a child feels safe, learning flourishes. If a child feels at risk, cognitive collapse occurs and learning stops. Body language communicates ninety-two percent of our message. We read eyes and hear tone and assess intentions. We will revisit emotion again shortly as we dig into video games. You know when you walk in the room whether your child is happy or your spouse is angry. You position yourself accordingly to receive their message. Children in a classroom are reading their teachers the same way, sensing a positive valence in a classroom—or not.

Todd Rose, named one of the Top Twenty Bright Minds in Boston to Watch, speaks to the natural variability among our children and reminds us that what is good for the children in the margins is good for all children, remembering also that variability is driven by context. Give each child a chance to work at his own level, at his own pace, in his own way, and build competence and confidence through success. Research tells us seventeen negative encounters in a day sets a child up for clinical depression. Many children encounter disapproval regularly from teachers who still think learning only happens while sitting still, paying attention, and reading the same textbook at the same time on the same topic. Todd Rose guides teachers in how to capitalize on media to enrich their message and how to help parents manage living in digital environments at home.

Electronic books have a place in our homes and in our classrooms—for reasons beyond individual platforms. They can be cost effective, space savers and readily updated with current information. Electronic media is here to stay. While some folks still grab the *Wall Street Journal* off their front porch or at the newsstand, many are logging on and getting news as soon as it happens, instead of as soon as it's printed.

What about Traditional Books?

Before you think I got one iPad lesson from a six-year-old and became a completely digital Grammy, let's go back to the science and its implications for reading. While digital sources are here to stay, they aren't likely to replace printed media altogether. A child connects to the very hungry caterpillar in Eric Carle's vibrantly illustrated picture book and its beautiful tissue paper art by touching the pages and putting little fingers in the holes as the caterpillar eats through the watermelon and the sausage and the strawberry ice cream, working its way, day by day, to emerge as a beautiful butterfly. In the same way, our nascent learners work through their mastery by eating a lesson at a time to bloom in front of our very eyes if we feed them carefully along their journey of learning.

But My Teen's Playing Video Games, Not Reading E-books

The excitement builds as we move from e-books, electronic files, sometimes enhanced with hyperlinks, to more animated content that often differs from books only in the methods of purchase and information delivery. Video games, on the other hand, are candy-colored cartoons where the child becomes the master of the universe in one swipe. They get hooked on the thrill of this power early. Look at two-year-olds: ninety-two percent of them are playing video games. Jane McGonigal, director of game research and development at the Institute for the Future, points out that the average teen has logged more than ten-thousand hours of media by graduation from high school, and fewer than ten-thousand hours in a classroom. She quickly adds that this secondary parallel education is a clarion call to pay attention to the new crop of digital learners who populate our classrooms today.

What have game designers learned that educators have forgotten? Why do video games hold a learner's attention, when our classrooms are losing it? How can we use the paradigm of the video game to inform education and inspire students? And what does that mean to you as a parent as you try to regulate your teen's screen time?

Harnessing the Power of Games for Good

McGonigal is a harbinger of the movement "to harness the power of games for good." She is convinced—and we are certainly seeing evidence—that games can inspire and reward, promote collaboration on an unimaginable scale, and keep gamers engaged at higher levels of challenge for longer periods of time than any other learning environment we have witnessed.

She sees this large-scale collaborative effort as the promise to solve the big problems in our global world. Gamers can merge their expertise, test their creative stamina, becoming powerful thinking partners for good, reaching for solutions that have previously overwhelmed masterminds in multiple disciplines. Who plays video games today? They come in all ages, at all levels, from all domains and they work together, undaunted by failure, exhilarated by challenge, in a social network that connects expansive networks of brain power as we have never before experienced.

McGonigal summarizes these digital games as "a way of thinking, a way of working together to accomplish real change, a platform to enable the future." She cites multiple examples of the power of collaboration to solve a daunting problem, demonstrating the collective might of synergy. There is exciting magic happening in the video game community, no doubt. Do they mean we should all throw away our books—even our e-books—and just start gaming? Of course not.

The Components of Digital Magic

As human beings, we want to engage and feel optimistic about our abilities. We have just investigated how invigorating and validating responsive relationships are for learning. McGonigal unpacks the power of digital games, and it goes beyond the visual appeal and the ability to control characters: games energize and engage; gamers work toward solutions. They set a goal and go after it. Gamers fail eighty percent of the time to meet their goal—not finishing a mission, not achieving a score—but they still keep going. Anything is possible to a gamer. They remain optimistic about their ability to reach their goal.

Optimism has the proven power to conquer learned helplessness. Author and psychologist Martin Seligman has chronicled this phenomenon in extensive research over the past decades. Carol Dweck, professor of psychology at Stanford University, builds on Seligman's research, confirming the significance of a growth mindset for building stamina and perseverance.

Gaming is seventy-five percent collaborative. It is a platform for trying something new, pulling on creative agency, and seeing the impact. Research tells us that emotion drives learning and relationships, and McGonigal demonstrates how gaming pulls on positive emotions: joy, relief, surprise, pride, curiosity, excitement, awe, wonder, contentment, creativity. Gaming produces positive stress, fierce determination. Gamers have perseverance. They experience Mihaly Csikszentmihalyi's proverbial "flow"—which he describes as the psychology of optimal experience, remaining immersed at the edge of their ability—exactly where Vygotsky said learning occurs, in their Zone of Proximal Development.

The Physiological Effects of Gaming

As a result of the instinctive release of hormones that appear to elevate energy to handle changing emotions, physiological changes happen in the body. McGonigal's work reveals that elevated levels of oxytocin occur. She points to our biology: heart rate increases, blood flow escalates, eyes dilate, nostrils even flare. These changes sound familiar. Remember the stress response we discussed in Chapter Five? What we are witnessing here is the positive stress that strengthens learning. Gamers have agency and experience this stress as enthusiasm, motivation to achieve.

Again, as parents, what does this mean for our teens? What types of educational environments or opportunities do we need to seek out for them? When we are involved in parent-teacher organizations or have other roles in our schools, what do we advocate, based on our new appreciation of video games? Not an arcade, but education based on the same cognition-enhancing attributes of video games. What would this look like?

Schools Could Work More Like Games

Take the test as many times as you want until you are happy with your score, just as gamers play the level until they get the score they want. Make school about mastery and competence, not about the score. Reports from the MacArthur Foundation's research are revealing that students learn more by taking tests over and over until they like their score, rather than spending more time studying for the test. This process helps learning happen. In video games, ordinary people do bold things and make history. School projects can connect to the world of transformative technology and create assignments that invite collaboration, looking to solve global challenges collectively. McGonigal cites how the challenge of protein folds that baffled scientists for years was solved in months by thousands of bloggers from around the globe working together. Learning occurs when assignments are relevant and interactive.

Games are collaborative; they connect people all over the world. We can develop academic projects that connect learners around the world, as well. We are at the cusp of change. Teachers at the head of the classroom are no longer the purveyors of all knowledge; they come in all sizes, shapes and ages on the world wide Web. With transformative technology and an information explosion, content is everywhere and readily available. Learners can unite and tackle the problems we need to solve around the globe.

One point of caution is that the digital brains in our classrooms can pose a challenge to teachers who are not as adept at navigating digital environments as readily as their students. What an exciting time to be a learner, and what a challenging time to be an educator. What an exhilarating time to discover the power of collaboration and bring us all together as a community of learners, combining the zeal of youthful discovery with the wisdom of age and experience.

Teachers and Parents Get a New Seat on the Bus

Let's go back to that idea that imbalances in fluency with digital navigation can change the dynamic of relationships between teens and their parents and teachers. Does this mean we just let them drive the bus? Not at all. But it does mean we need to adapt our roles according to the realities of the world we all live in. Redefining these relationships brings together many of the concepts we have been discussing.

Once again, neuroscience research confirms that emotion drives learning. Positive emotion, anticipatory sets of success, relevant curriculum, supportive behavior, guided teaching are the fodder for learning. Communicating support in body language and in words sets the emotional climate for positive learning to occur. Guided teaching, leading a student (of any size, shape or age) through relevant learning works. Believing in our teens even before they believe in themselves is the foundation for healthy brain development. Our roles in their lives are as important as ever, but we need to look at ourselves as mentors and guides rather than lecturers. In order to instill our children with our values and important information in a healthy, successful way, we need to fully engage them in the acquisition of the information. As we saw happening in the internships in Chapter Three, learning rarely happens "because I say so." That's the quickest way to lose a person's attention, at any age. What works better? Here's an example:

My five-year-old granddaughter burst in the kitchen door, covered in damp soil and filled with glee. Paysan shouted, "Lochlan just found a salamander! We need to google salamander to see what to feed it! Hurry!" Dashing for the computer, she had quickly sounded out the s-a-l and called out, "Grammy, how do you spell salamander! Quick! It's so hungry!" This ardent desire for a new spelling word is Eagleman's just-in-time learning personified. Content is everywhere. Switching from just-in-case learning to just-in-time learning—and tying it to past learning—builds the case for changing to a growth mindset in education and parenting.

My three-year-old grandson carries his iTouch in his backpack. I told him I would play a game with him, but I couldn't get it to go to the right screen. Hale looked up at me with a twinkle. "Silly, Grammy. Push this first. You have to turn it on!" Then he showed me how to move the Mario brothers to their destinations. Yes, we need to adapt our roles!

So What's the Downside?

Growing up with media can provide enrichment and enhance the lessons parents seek to impart to their children. However, common sense dictates that too much of anything can have a negative impact. You can capitalize on the glories of technology to entertain and use these sensory stimuli to build on the universal lessons that will help your children flourish. Or you can succumb to the dazzling distraction and turn your teenagers over to the electronic milieu, which can then become a primary source of information that may carry adverse unintended consequences. How you include media in your family dynamic can influence whether media enriches or exploits your children's development.

Parents are their children's first and best teachers. Children learn early from their parents—important lessons in vocabulary, emotion, and attitude—the building blocks of later resilience. Parents look for ways to enhance cognitive development in their progeny. Books remain a constant learning device, but electronic media has altered the way children perceive their world, replacing—or, in many instances, significantly modifying—the role of teacher historically held by the parent and extended family.

Worried parents and grandparents are asking probing questions about the impact media consumption might have on the architecture of developing brains. Speculation is gradually being informed by empirical research—though this research is challenging to gather and to interpret fairly—that can help investigate the impact of electronic media on the cognitive, emotional, social, and behavioral development in children. While this new delivery system of entertainment can augment and even transform education for the better, it can also render children vulnerable as the networks deliver young innocents to aggressive advertisers.

Media research can help us teach our teens how to navigate the confusing issues that confront them as they are pummeled by media options calling out for their attention. Teens can learn how to garner the positive aspects for growth and development that widespread digital media provides, while eschewing the hazards that can introduce imbalance—and even harm—into their world.

The Perils of Over-Consumption

One of the most alarming revelations from the robust literature in media research is the amount of time children and adolescents devote to media consumption. Children aged two to eighteen average three hours watching television, one hour listening to music, one hour playing computer games each day. Children from eight to eighteen increase the hours in each category, statistically moving up to six hours per day; when overlapping media is used simultaneously—instant messaging and tweeting while working on the computer with the television on in the background—the hours increase to over eight per day. The average time for reading per day is forty-four minutes. This immersion in media can have some positive educational components, but the potential for negative consequences begs caution at all levels.

Certainly, effective educational media has capitalized on how experience and enrichment trigger innate genetic predisposition. Some thoughtfully developed programs and games use the tools regularly which foster learning in their media lessons for their pre-school audience, scaffolding nascent learners with interesting language, compelling music, stimulating colors, and engaging adults who use dynamic and fast-paced visual context to build meaningful language and number skills for viewers.

Jean Piaget, the renowned Swiss developmental psychologist and philosopher, pointed out the way children observe and interpret quantity in his famous theory of conservation. He had children view the same amounts of orange juice: one presented in a tall, thin container, the other in a short, wide container. Piaget demonstrated that reason can, ultimately, triumph over perception when a child reaches the developmental stage that allows him or her to see that the amounts remain the same, even though the shape of the vessel might suggest that the taller contained the larger amount of liquid. Experience can trigger genes, building on what is innate in a child and moving a nascent investigator toward comprehending concepts such as reversible functions in math. Building on Piaget's research, Sesame Street has developed a curriculum that supports and enriches a child's natural learning curve and can, therefore, become an important building block for helping young children have reason triumph over perception. The show uses creative technology and procedures for effective teaching, processes that could inform parents as they formulate their own teaching methods for their children, pulling on positive features in media to build a base for learning.

Currently, educational neuroscience can inform parents about children's learning by elucidating the development of mental representations, a process by which neural networks in the brain use electrochemical activity to code information. This process can be observed in laboratory settings using noninvasive devices, such as the functional MRI, to track stimuli responses to distinct regions of the brain, giving alert researchers a window into how executing a particular task activates a particular area of the brain and, thus, providing clues about how learning occurs.

This new research can be used either to enrich or to exploit youngsters exposed to repeated presentations, depending on the goal of the presenter. While learning vocabulary and math concepts may be positive, selling a product may not be in the best interest of a child or his health. We are seeing the beginning of more widespread recognition of this impact: the abundance of commercials for sugar-coated cereal and other unhealthy foods that permeate children's viewing time are now becoming the subject of legislation. Mental representations and technology can produce brain scans that will be useful in understanding how the brain handles information, but limitations still remain. Individual differences in processing strategies can vary, and different technologies offer specific interpretive data so vigilance must prevail to match the research instrument to the question at hand.

Overlapping exposure to media with child development and learning leads to issues of concern about how children react at different stages to potentially destructive forces, such as violence and aggression—both of which they can encounter in electronic media. Children can be at risk emotionally from viewing content that is not age appropriate. Research indicates that aggression may be a learned response. If so, then exposure to overtly aggressive and violent acts through television and video games is troublesome news.

Choosing Media

Family viewing habits, as well as family communication patterns, can vary. Parents should consider reviewing standards for evaluation of appropriate media for their children as they set family patterns for viewing. Alert parents should seek personal training in how to decipher a website and then teach their children how to do the same. Parents owe it to their children to help them become discerning consumers of media.

Media research can temper speculation and supply documented information to give parents confidence in their choices for their children's time investment in media consumption. Yet definitive answers are hard to find. Research is challenging to compile, and research methods have limitations. Intuitive judgments may not be grounded in empirical data.

The most important finding that recurs among the rich literature available about children and what they hold onto from visual stimuli relates directly to the amount of engagement that occurs among family members, especially between a parent and a child. Parents who watch and play video games alongside their children can proffer their opinions, using the moment of engagement for genuine learning about personal values and about how to use time in the most efficient manner.

Parents face a serious challenge: they are responsible for monitoring the quality and quantity of the visual stimuli their children encounter. When your teen was younger, watching together, playing together, and evaluating together were the best methods for handling the potential for misinterpretation. Being aware of what teens are viewing and engaging with them about it still helps. If you watch a video with them and you see messages that you know are harmful, mention it. Talk to your teen respectfully about the consequences of the behavior you are observing. Guide her to a deeper understanding of the situation, much as you guided her to learn the tricks of solving a jig-saw puzzle when she was little. Teens do not get the same messages from media as an adult who brings a different experiential base to the viewing. Learning happens best in meaningful relationships. Passive viewing does not garner the same lessons. Interaction remains the best environment for positive learning and growing healthy brains.

Neuro-Parenting Principles
CHAPTER EIGHT

1. Reading can build meaningful relationships that can foster brain development.
2. Reading can enrich emotional language and appreciation of art.
3. Reading provides the foundation for developing language skills and higher test scores.
4. Media is providing a new platform for learning and holds enormous potential.
5. Electronic books have advantages: quick updates, convenient, can offer scaffolding.
6. Education can learn from video games.
7. Optimism can conquer learned helplessness.
8. Too much of anything is not usually good for us.

GETTING
INTO THE
RIGHT
COLLEGE

While understanding teens' brains can help us guide them to maximum success, we cannot use the scientific truths of the human brain as tools for our own ego gratification. Each teen's maximum success is defined by his unique genetic makeup, not by his parents, not by his family history, his neighborhood, his school or his college counselor. Our job, as parents, educators and college counselors, is to help him find the definition of success that uniquely suits him and have the experiences that make it most possible to obtain it. If we use this knowledge like Pygmalion, or Dr. Frankenstein, to create children to meet our own needs rather than to nurture and support the full potential of their genetic flourish, we fail them. It is important to use our knowledge of neuroscience to help our teens get into the right college. It is more important to use our knowledge of our teens to define what that right college might be.

I firmly hold that many of the important truths that neuroscience points out for children, teens, parents, and all people are fundamentally similar to some of the pearls of wisdom traditionally espoused by my grandmother. Having the insights and empirical data of the researchers in these pages proves that parts of her message were correct: relationships, reading, nutrition, sleep, and balance are all still important, maybe even more so in these hectic times. But now we have irrefutable evidence that ignoring these components of a healthy life can actually lead to poor cognitive development, disease, and, in advanced cases, death. The human brain, even in all its remarkable adaptability and phenomenal plasticity, still has limits. And we need to recognize and respect them if we want our teens to reach the highest levels of their genetic potential.

So how do we use all the information we have about the brain to help our children succeed? Does modern life—the conveniences, the devices, the speed, the independence—offer us better, faster ways to become super-parents rearing super-children and sending super-teens on to higher and higher levels of success? Or does it mean that we are more challenged than ever in being able to obtain healthy balance in our lives—our bodies, our homes, our schools—and therefore our societies? Whenever mankind makes a discovery, there are those who will use it for good, and those who will use it for personal benefit, denying or ignoring the cost.

Success starts at home. The well-adjusted child moves into the school system that nurtures her mind, challenges her to grow and prepares her for life—socially, intellectually, spiritually and physically. At every stage, the community supports this healthy development, wanting only the best for this child, so that she can in turn know herself and give her best back to the community. It sounds so simple.

Of course, it isn't. The path is fraught with competition and pitfalls. Fear permeates the system, and rumors swirl: if my child doesn't go to this preschool, he won't get into this independent school, this college, this grad school, this prestigious firm. Failure at any level is not an option. Obviously, everyone can't grow up to be the president of the U.S., and Wall Street isn't big enough to hold all of our children. But isn't that a good thing?

The diverse opportunities of our world require adults with diverse skill sets. Each one of our children is uniquely suited for a different type of success. It holds, then, that we need to look at our own concept of success—both academic and personal—as we prepare each child for adulthood. Most importantly, we need to remember that success is a journey that does not end with college admissions or even college graduation. Throughout their school years, we need to keep our focus directly on the real reasons we are educating our children in the first place.

Rethinking Our Goals and Methods

Who are the learners? Who owns the learning? What is mastery, and what do we need to master anyway? Children learn through exploration. Failure is the portal to discovery. They can get it wrong and keep going. Children arrive with a positive spirit of discovery and adventure. Learning is a verb, a process, and understanding gained through trial and error.

With the focus of our education system on codification, competition, and comparison—not to mention standardized testing—children go to school, where they learn rules for success in this "get into a selective college" game. These rules can stifle the very spirit that we seek to ignite. I question the rules, especially when I see escalating numbers of young children taking Ritalin, Cylert or Vivance. One independent school report-ed thirty-nine percent of its lower school children were on neurocognitive enhancers, which have also become the drug of choice that many teens borrow from their friends as they go in to take their SAT tests. Not a good idea. While some children will profit from using these stimulants to fo-cus, many children might prosper if school officials could rethink whether classroom expectations are age-appropriate. And science has proven to us that children develop at their own pace, so we might need to toss out or at least broaden the concept of age-appropriate.

As long as standardized test scores drive curriculum and we measure success only by an academic metric at a predetermined pace (and define the quality of the school accordingly), children will be vulnerable and at risk of turning off. I watched an independent school regularly dismiss children who had not mastered reading by the end of kindergarten, saying they were not fodder for their enriched program that prided itself on having their students measure a grade level or two higher than students in peer institutions. Measured by what metric? By whose priority? For whose good? Those dismissed from the program were often boys, often with summer birthdays.

Neuroscience and grandmother's wisdom concur wholeheartedly: chil-dren grow sequentially, at their own pace. You cook a pound cake longer than an angel food cake, and both are delicious. Every child "cooks" in a time that is right for his unique genetic makeup. When we push them beyond their normal capacity—even adding perceived extenders like drugs—we need to pause, catch our breath, and ask ourselves what we are doing to our children. Each child is important and too valuable to lose. We need to honor each child as an individual statistic, pulling that child's story off the dashboard of data. We need to grow that child, help-ing him find his place, tell his story. A few bold schools are beginning to see the light. If we all remain focused on changing the system to serve the learners, without doubt we will improve our world. But in the mean-time, you're getting concerned about getting your teen into college.

Navigating the Frenzied Waters of College Admissions

Why Has Getting Into College Become So Confusing, Complicated and Competitive?

Over recent years, the number of graduating high-school seniors has gone from 2.1 million per year to 3.3 million. The appearance of the electronic application has made it much easier for more students to apply to more schools, increasing the average number of applications filed by each student from five to twelve. Much of this increase has been directed at the fewer than fifty of the three-thousand-plus colleges in America that have the luxury of accepting fewer than half of their applicants. Yet the number of "seats" at those schools has remained essentially flat. Also, with recent changes in visas allowing students to remain longer in the United States, international applicants have surged in numbers, a significant factor increasing applicant pools.

In addition, in 2007, William Fitzsimmons, the dean of Undergraduate Admissions and Financial Aid at Harvard University, launched a movement to redistribute financial aid to make Harvard more accessible to more people, announcing the roll-out of a new Financial Aid Initiative. This Initiative stated that any family making up to $60,000—and currently the number has increased to $65,000—will not have to pay tuition at Harvard, with more help, too, for families with up to $180,000 in annual income. These efforts, quickly adopted by others, threw open the doors at these most selective schools to populations which previously self-selected out of applying. The result is a surge in activity amidst a system in flux. Never in the history of the United States have so many applied so often to so few schools.

Why You Should Help Your Teen With The Application Process

Some say that students should drive the college process themselves with no outside help or influence. Certainly, we would hope that ideal were the case. We would also hope that every student and adult would follow a proper diet and exercise regularly, yet obesity rates soar. Twenty years and more than three thousand students later—plus the experience of going through this process with my own three children—I can attest that most seniors in high school are anxious about this process.

Just as brain science can show us how best to nurture our teen's brain, it can also explain to us why the college application process can make even the calmest home suddenly erupt in drama. And sometimes it can create more than just drama. Emotional overflow from perceived stress can trigger regressive behaviors that can create a developmental crisis. The tension between current abilities and future aspirations can lead teens to experience a nagging feeling of incompetence and uncertainty. This kind of stress over a prolonged period of time can kill neurons, destroy brain cells in the hippocampus, and trigger depression.

Breakthroughs in neuroscience reinforce our innate realization: adolescents profit from help—as do their parents—when high stakes decisions about college are at hand. Adolescent brains are not yet fully developed. In teen brains, the amygdala is more dominant in processing emotional information, particularly at volatile moments, when a teen feels overwhelmed or when challenge morphs into threat and a teen can be thrown into the stress response that we talked about in Chapter Five, potentially triggered by the negative feedback loops built into the application process itself. Add the burdens of sleep deprivation to the mix—many adolescents are averaging seven hours or less, when they may need nine—and judgment can be seriously skewed. In part, teens feel vulnerable to a college admission system about which they perceive they have little control over outcome.

Anger can also accompany this process. Many parents feel it, and it makes sense. The anger is real. You, too, ride an emotional roller coaster when your teen applies to college. Your child is leaving the nest; you are about to make a substantial investment in real money and time; and you, too, cannot control the outcome in an amorphous process that lacks transparency even if for a good reason.

College admission officers must fill their beds, meet budget projections, honor institutional objectives, and shape a class of learners. They are challenged to be strategic about their admission criteria and crystal-clear about their goals, all the while recognizing that any irrelevant demands or additional questions from their side could be a possible tipping point that could topple an anxious teen applicant already overwhelmed by how to handle the process. College folks seek to balance access and affordability, recognizing their pivotal role in preserving a flourishing democracy.

Changing Demographics

The United States was in a post baby-boomlet, with escalating numbers of high-school graduates until two years ago. Declining numbers will bottom out in five years, but while the numbers will be back up by 2020, the college population will be different. The economic recession, which sent many non-traditional students seeking career changes back to college; the redistribution of financial aid, which will provide more access to first generation students; and the explosion of international candidates represent major factors in the shifting demographic. Many colleges are less equipped to manage these populations and will have to adjust accordingly.

The current emphasis on rankings reflects a consumer mentality. The perception that education is becoming something you purchase to get the best job can cause a student to fall prey to seeking the best ranked school, eschewing the more appropriate target: finding the best fit for personal growth—the best place to become a critical thinker, a discerning consumer, a problem solver, an interesting person. This misperception adds to the confusion about how to choose a college.

The Role of Independent Counselors

Do you need to hire an independent counselor in addition to the school's college counselor? Many parents now tackle the college application process by calling in an independent consultant as a reliable, well-informed, thinking partner because the process is complicated, competitive, and confusing. Independent consultants can help students navigate this important developmental milestone and help parents connect with their own perceptions and hidden agendas, preserving family relationships along this challenging journey of self-discovery.

The proper role of a college counselor—be they employed by schools or parents—is to encourage self-awareness and discovery while maximizing fit. That process takes time, and time is a commodity in the shortest of supply for counselors at schools where ratios often are over five hundred, six hundred, even a thousand students for one counselor. Given difficult economic times, and until policy makers or school leadership can find the funding and commitment to train new advisers, those ratios will worsen. In this environment, there is an appropriate role for properly motivated, well-trained, and credentialed independent consultants.

When you introduce a neutral and trusted adult, even when your teen's school has a college counseling staff where ratios may appear more reasonable, you can help keep the balance in your family. Many parents—out of love for their child—become overly consumed with achievement. Without even realizing it, they can be covertly delivering this message to their teens and can be driving their children relentlessly in pursuit of a prestigious college admission that may not be the best fit for personal growth.

The independent consultant can provide the extra time and guidance needed for many parents to reconcile their own feelings about achievement, as well as to help quell the fear of failure and disappointment that many students anticipate if they do not earn admission to the schools which they perceive they should enter for future career stability and social mobility. Again, science reveals that teens and their parents need help; schools are challenged to provide that extra support. Independent consultants have a role to play. As adults, we can model for teens the strength of collaboration for positive outcome as they move through the college application process.

Achievement Mania

Intense focus on early achievement is, perhaps, cascading down from the competitive state of college admissions. Nervous parents and anxious teens ask me questions like, "Mrs. Muir, how many hours of community service will it take for me to get into Stanford?" Parents perceive that starting early to build an athlete or a virtuoso will give a child a competitive edge in the race to a selective college. Well, yes. Colleges do reward those who focus early and achieve a level of excellence or quantify lofty contributions by using the personal gifts they have been given in service to others. And science confirms the use-it-or-lose-it mentality. But how much is too much, and how early is too early?

I exert considerable effort protecting many children from their parents' urge to force an identity on them for the sake of puffing up a college resume. Many parents get tangled up in this prickly mania, defining their own success, or failure, by the college to which their children are accepted. We need to spend more time understanding our children's intelligence and discovering opportunities that enhance it and, eventually, colleges where it will thrive and flourish. Ultimately, this approach will provide your child with the greatest number of options and the best chance of success. Pressuring teens into a preconceived definition of success or college choice is backwards and, in the long run, can prove destructive to them.

Children Spend Their First Ten Years Figuring Out How; the Next Ten, Why

We have been investigating the message of neuroscience about how important experience is in turning on a child's genes. So the healthy approach is to expose a child to a smorgasbord of options: lacrosse, basketball, volleyball, tennis, swimming, piano, violin, painting—just not all in the same year, not all before age six, and not when academic foundations are getting grounded in a long day at school. Children need unstructured time for creative play. Children and teens have the same stress response system as adults. Organized time can quickly squeeze out creative playtime—an equally important component of development. Children spend their first ten years figuring out how, and their second ten years figuring out why. Both pursuits demand down time for processing and developing.

Richard Weissbourd, a widely respected child and family psychologist on the faculty at Harvard University, warns that parents need to deal with their own irrational feelings about achievement to escape the temptation to measure the value of their children by the level of their achievement, academic or otherwise. He points out that children derive their sense of high achievement and why it is significant from their parents. And parents can deliver mixed messages.

Emotional Problems Cross Demographic Lines

Suniya Luthar, researcher at Columbia University, is documenting that emotional problems cross demographic lines, impacting both children of poverty and children of privilege, with the latter group three times more likely to report clinical levels of depression. Children who see achievement failures as personal failures are at the highest risk. Achievement pressure can permeate families and school communities, often fed by the perception that getting into the most impressive college is the only road to the best career, the most money, the happiest life. The right answer: finding the college that's right for the individual—determined by personal investigation and introspection—is the best preparation for a developing a productive career and meaningful relationships over time.

Children Need Time

Teens need the time to figure out who they are and discover their own unique aptitudes. They need to discover their passion and then develop it through appropriate experiences that are matched to them. So often I see it happening in reverse: well-meaning parents become aggressive, cluttering up their children's lives with resume-building activities that have nothing to do with the child's interests or aptitudes.

Yet parents know their children better than anyone else. So how can you best help your teen? Be an active listener, an engaged thinking partner, who can help guide her to the experiences that will help unfold her natural talents. Once again: *Genes load the gun. Experience pulls the trigger.*

Weissbourd relates stories about strung-out achievement junkies and parents who drive them relentlessly. The race to the right college has turned many loving parents into paramilitants who pummel their children with hollow lists of superficial activities thinking their children will be more competitive with longer lists of activities. But the lack of depth in any activity prevents a child from really discovering innate talents or deep interests—and doesn't enrich his story as he seeks the attention of an admission officer and a seat at the college. Victim mentality can set in. We all need to keep in mind that these are offices of admissions, not offices of rejection.

Over-programming with activities, even with good intentions, compromises—sometimes almost cuts out—the creative play that is a child's work. Play is where he learns how to deal with others to lay the foundations for later friendships and working relationships. It is where he learns to live with himself and discover how the world works. Bugs and water play, the kinds of things a child can do in the backyard are where the beginning tenets of exploration and discovery start. This type of discovery should continue as the child becomes a teenager and even an adult. Employers tell me they see new employees with stellar resumes who are rigid with formulas and who have limited experience with fluid intelligence. *All Grown Up and Nowhere to Go*, *The Race to Nowhere*, *Crazy Busy*, *Grand Theft Childhood*, *Nurture Shock*—these titles and others with similar messages line our bookshelves and give us a clue about perils of overscheduling our children.

Inadvertently, we can guilt children by making careless remarks, often with good intentions. I was standing in back of the chain-link fence of the dugout, when my seven-year-old grandson bounded up to me flashing a dollar bill for me to hold for him while he got ready to bat in his championship game. "My coach just gave it to me for catching a fly ball. If we hit a home run, we get FIVE dollars!" I could see that winning was important. My jaw dropped, but I remained silent. What would you say? How would you react? How do we incentivize a child to adopt our agenda?

Carrots and Sticks

It's important to take the time to sort out your feelings about achievement before your teen begins the college admissions process. What do power and status and money mean in your family? What are your real dreams for your teen, and what are the goals you are consciously and subconsciously pushing him toward? How do you believe her success reflects on you? How do we nurture self-regulation, encourage good behavior, and help children navigate other's intentions?

Weissbourd writes about the parents we mean to be, describing how the message we intend to communicate can get scrambled. Spanking is a good example. A frustrated parent may intend to use a spanking to change a young child's behavior, thinking it will teach the child not to do that again. But what the child actually learns from the spanking is that it is okay to hit someone who disagrees with you. And even more damaging: it is okay to hit someone you love.

Getting Good Essays

When a teen invites me in to the inner sanctum of his soul, I tread lightly and move ahead with both respect and awe. Teens will often let you in, if you are lucky, if you listen, really listen, and can earn their trust. They are astute, these teens; they know when you really care about them. This moment of self-reflection is an important developmental milestone. They are soul-searching. They are catching a glimpse of who they might be. Sometimes we fill our life with distraction to dim the still small voice inside. It's a scary place to go. No one can write a better essay than a teen who backs off and listens.

Dr. Frances Jensen, professor of neurology at Harvard Medical School, says that teens are not adults with low mileage. They care and feel deeply. They can be soulful, and they can see through façade. They are brutally honest. Even behind those nice Southern manners or that New England reserve, there is an observant young man just waiting to see if he can trust you with his deepest thoughts.

We must catch ourselves when we are tempted to force our own perception of what a child should do or become by letting our opinion come out and suffocate or interrupt a moment of light for a teen who is searching his thoughts for a college essay. Every child has a moving college essay inside, just as every adult probably has one good commencement address inside—you just have to coax it out, often by asking probing questions.

The journey of self-discovery that the college application process prompts is fraught with anxiety, riddled with apprehension, and primed for joy. For the student who pauses, who is courageous enough to put himself out there and discover himself, the reward is not the email or fat envelope that arrives, but the way he feels when he pushes "submit." He knows he is worthy. He has discovered that he has something special to take to a college to enrich its community. There is more than one place to find happiness and learn to become a productive adult; that's a hard lesson to learn amidst the achievement frenzy that our teens dodge every single day.

When we stop defining children's worth by their academic achievement and the college sweatshirt we wear, and treasure their good deeds and kind thoughts, we push them further toward success than any enrichment agenda can.

Test Scores

Begun by the military to determine who to send out into the field and who to train, test scores have become a staple of our existence and a measuring stick for our children. While standardized tests can be a useful tool to assess where a child is on the road to mastery by isolating those gaps in skills that need more attention, test scores have now become a label that children listen for, self-describe as, and live up to—for both good and bad.

A WPPSI score on a three-year-old as a predictor of future academic success is risky at best. What it doesn't tell you about your child is equal to what it might reveal. It is more a report card on parenting to date than a projection about potential. Working memory is a far stronger predictor of academic success than an IQ score any day.

Putting it in Perspective

It's natural to be nervous about college admissions. Here's what I'd like you and your teen to remember:

Explore your options.
Make careful choices that keep
   your options open.
Be vigilant.

Enjoy each other.
Manage the process without
   falling for the hype.
Stay whole.

A particular journalist I respect who follows breaking events in education pulled me aside at a national conference one day to ask me a question about a prickly issue we were both working to resolve. He reminded me that journalists have to write stories that grab attention. Even fair-minded journalists like him had to find the edgy stories that would lure readers. Media hype draws readers who want to be informed, entertained, and surprised. Be a discerning consumer, and put everything you read and hear in context.

Guiding teens through the college application process for well over two decades now, I know that there is a hidden side to it that doesn't get much press. I have witnessed remarkable stories of self-discovery. Applications require you to tell your story. Few times in our lives do we have the luxury to pause and reflect about where we have been, and become strategic about where we are heading. Working closely with these creative, amazing teens, I have watched them come into an understanding of themselves that is worth as much, perhaps, as anything they will subsequently learn in college. Listen to what just a few of them have discovered mattered to them:

Values

This summer we celebrated my grandfather's eightieth birthday. I watched my grandfather's eyes light up as he opened his presents. My mind flashed back. When I was younger, my grandfather would pick me up, plop me down on his knee, and tell me that I was bound for greatness. He would tell me how lucky I was to have the intellect and character of a man destined for success. He would go on and on about how I could become a doctor, an astronaut or even the president of the United States. When I was a carefree and insouciant eight-year-old, these words had little impact on me, except for the entertainment value that I received from watching my grandfather's eyes light up with hope, promise, and pride. As I grew older, I began to understand that regardless of the extent of my personal talents, the success of my future rested upon how I applied these gifts. The responsibility was mine. Since that epiphany years ago, I have studied people that I most respected, trying to emulate their positive qualities. I watched my grandfather and saw a man of love and passion. I looked at my dad and saw a leader full of determination. I listened to my scoutmaster and understood his honor and his devotion to integrity. After years of watching, admiring, imitating, testing, and perfecting, I am beginning to understand what an admirable adult is all about. I want to lift my grandson on to my knee someday and tell him what he can become. Then I want him to be able to look at me with the same respect, honor, and love that I felt as an eight-year-old on my grandfather's knee.

Family

I had always thought of my family as being rather adventurous, but when my father announced just two weeks prior the start of my sixth-grade year that he had sold the house and we were going to live on our boat, I thought that my family had crossed the line from adventurous to downright crazy. As I sat for the last time in our spacious living room, I thought about life in cramped quarters with my parents and three brothers, and I wondered about the strain of living in such a restrictive environment.

We had always been a close family who liked travel and adventure. As a family, we had managed to squash into a tent on a camping trip in the hill country and to sleep six people in one hotel room at Disney World. But those times had lasted only a night or two, and this new adventure was to last four or five months. When moving day arrived, I watched in disbelief as our material possessions, seemingly gone forever, were packed into a moving truck. As the truck drove away, I began to dread what was ahead.

During the five months on the boat with my brothers, I began to see them in new ways, developing special relationships with each of them. Price, the oldest, at six-foot-three, had a tough time adjusting to the limitations of a boat and its tiny cabins. Matt, second youngest, was known as the bathroom beauty. A big-time fourth-grader, Matt spent at least a half-hour in the bathroom every morning trying to look as good as possible for the girls. Andrew, the youngest, was more concerned with eating than anything else. Standing four feet at the start of third grade, Andrew was convinced that his height (or lack thereof) was from not eating enough or drinking enough milk. Personally, I think Andrew was just sick of being stuffed into closets and shoved under beds. Nonetheless, despite our individual quirks and demands, what I remember most were the special times we all spent pulling together.

My most vivid memory is of the night that ten-year-old Andrew slipped, trying to board the boat. Inside with Matt and Price, I heard his frightened scream and splash as he crashed into the water. Darting up the stairwell to the deck of the boat, we jumped onto the dock and reached down to grab him. It took all three of us to pull a panicked Andrew out the water and onto the dock. Terrified of jellyfish and other unfriendly inhabitants of the water, Andrew screamed and flailed his arms, making his rescue even more difficult. When we finally pulled him out, the four of us sat on the dock, staring at each other. We didn't have to say a word because we were all thinking the same thing—we were thankful we still had each other.

Today we live in a comfortable home with a backyard and room to spread out. Yet things within our family have not really changed. Matt still spends hours in the bathroom, and we all still love to shove Andrew down laundry chutes. What has brought us close together though, besides hurried breakfasts and sit-down dinners, is scouting. When Andrew completes his project and earns his Eagle Scout Award, we will be four Eagle Scouts. Since Price's Eagle project five years ago, as a family, we have rallied to the aid and support of each other. When Price was having problems with volunteers, Matt, Andrew, and I joined him, and we went door-to-door collecting clothing and blankets for a shelter. Two years later, as I was struggling to pour eleven tons of gravel over a half-mile trail at the arboretum, Price returned the favor by showing up with four of his friends who saw the eleven-ton problem as a light workout. With his body-builders, we finished the job by the end of the day. Most recently, we joined forces when Matt launched his project to collect two-thousand English and Spanish books for a local school that did not have a library. After local press coverage and a few articles, Matt had no problem finding people who wanted to donate, so Price and I drove Matt and Andrew around the city for weeks, as Matt collected almost five-thousand books and over two-thousand dollars in donations.

What I have learned from scouting, those five months cramped on the boat, and everyday life is that the people I can count on are my brothers. There is a special bond that links us. I know whenever I am struggling, there is someone ready to help me. As brothers, we are a team four times as strong as any one of us. As a team, we will always be there to stuff Andrew down laundry chutes. But when he really needs us, we will also be there to pull him out of deep, jellyfish-infested waters.

Clarity

I watched the white towers meet their dusty doom on the ground in front of me. Once a grouping of monoliths piercing the sky, reduced now to just a hunk of twisted, scrap metal, flattened by the tremendous weight of one on top the next. The dust filled the air.

I looked around at the crowd that had gathered in the early morning hours of a remarkably arid Houston morning. The drone of the helicopter as it covered the event provided a morbid background for this gloomy day. The lady next to me, who I noticed was from the historical society, wept.

Two feet from her was the wiring for the detonation of the explosives. Upon inspection, it was not a plunger-type detonator, but rather a crude piece of wood, painted black with twenty nails in it. The nails went all the way through the board and were hooked to the lines that ran into the building on the other side. When the all-clear order was given, a tall man in a hard hat moved deftly, touching each nail with a cable connected to the end of a battery terminal. Instantaneously, explosions were both heard and felt.

The ground, at first, seemed to swallow the initial ten to twenty feet of the structures. As the metal reached its crushable limit, the towers slowly listed, and finally crashed down with a swirling cloud of dust and emotion.

Unlike the towers, I quietly broke into inner misery. Not destroyed by some man-made explosive device, but devastated by human emotion.

Pain coursed through my body, making my skin feel hot and my throat constrict in on my trachea. I felt coolness running down my face, and when I lifted my hand, I discovered that I was crying.

I had been a part of those towers; they were the rice elevators that my father had built. And since his passing, his memory has slipped further and further from my mind. I could see his face, projected onto the once radiant white surface. The voice of the past echoed in my ears and tainted my feelings on the destruction of the structures.

I learned from watching the destruction that early morning that not everything lasts. In fact, that not many things last—that the only way to truly hold onto something, is to entrust it to memory.

Character

My grandfather often told me that there is one, and only one, thing by which you can rightfully judge a man: his character. As he defined it, that is how a man holds himself in times when the sky is falling. I believe my grandfather's words to be true, for they fit all people, including me. My father also believes this to be true, but as more of an economist, he adds that a man of solid character has good credit. Good credit and good character mean that you make a promise, and you keep it. No excuses for not doing it; no matter how hard it may be, you make your payments. You keep your word.

My grandfather also taught me how to run a ranch. As a boy, I would ride around for hours with him in his old blue Chevy truck just finding the slope of the hill, popping the clutch into neutral and slowly rolling down as we talked about each cow that sauntered by. He knew every one of his cows, or his girls, as he called them; and after many years at his side, so did I.

By the time I was thirteen, I felt confident in my knowledge of our herd. I could by then recognize each of the six hundred cattle as well as my grandfather did, as well as I know my own family; I enjoyed following them over time as they turned from calf to heifer to cow. Soon I began envisioning a herd of my own; I wanted about fifty F-1 stripe mother cows, since this breed does well in Texas heat. I discussed with my father and grandfather the idea of my somehow buying my own herd, and after much conversation, we decided that I should try to take a loan from a bank.

The three of us travelled to the nearby town of Anderson to meet the bank's sole loan officer, Buck Cain. He thought it was an idea, not necessarily a good one, but an idea. Eventually, we cajoled and coaxed him into a loan agreement; with the guarantee of payment from my grandfather, the bank gave me a loan at one point over prime. Never mind my wounded pride, I was ecstatic. Now I had a chance to own my own herd and to build my own record of character and credit.

My girls arrived on a hellish day in August when the tormenting heat created an eerie haze. We vaccinated and ear-tagged them quickly. It was early morning and already the thermometer read ninety degrees; by noon the mercury would rise over one hundred. I wanted to release them to seek shade from the stressful heat. To make payments every quarter, I sold calves produced from those original fifty cows, and in this way over the past three years I have paid the bank a sum equivalent to the purchase of a large truck. Every payment has been made on time, except once when I asked for an extension due to a poor market following a summer drought.

My grandfather did not live long enough to see me kill the note. I am glad that he saw me on my way down the road to keeping my word. For much of his life, it didn't seem he had more than he wore, but he always had his integrity. He often told me that was all he needed. Character is what he preached. Taking the loan, I risked more than bad credit—I gambled with my grandfather's perception of me. I made a promise to him, and I kept it.

A Team Effort

At the core of this conversation about preparing our teens for college and success remains the need for us to hold on to a social conscience that pits idealism against pragmatism. Issues of equity, access, and transparency will continue to chase admission officers and independent consultants as, no doubt, will investigative reporters. That's as it should be since education transcends generations and is at the very foundation of our nation's economy, personal productivity, and quality of life.

I hope you now share my belief that teens need our help and our support to find themselves and their own inner drive, to provide them context and reference points to navigate the dizzying array of choices and freedoms that make America at once both great and challenging. Leading a student to the threshold of his own mind should be, at best, a team effort—for college and for life.

Neuro-Parenting Principles
CHAPTER NINE

1. Teens need to choose the college that is the right fit for them.
2. The sheer velocity of modern times can get teens off balance.
3. Each child is different; each brain is different.
4. College admission is competitive because more students are applying.
5. Parents can get caught up in the achievement mania and hurt their children.
6. A personal journey of self-discovery can help teens plan their future and make better choices based on personal reflection.
7. Adults and teens should work collaboratively; team spirit garners positive results in the college search, in life.

MY
HOPE
FOR MY
FAMILY
AND YOURS

As I watch my grandchildren perched on the edges of their nests, ready and eager for flight, I marvel at the possibilities that lay ahead for them, even as I shudder at how many barriers exist that could block their healthy brain development. I feel the winds of change blowing across the landscape, heralded by the information explosion and transformative technology that permeate our crazy, busy world.

I am writing with a sense of urgency, wondering how best to meet the needs of our children and prepare them for the world they will face. I write at the nexus of research and practice, knowing that we can get it right if we pause to think collaboratively and act appropriately. The problems the world will present our children and grandchildren are too big for one brain, for one discipline. So how can we arm them with the resilience they will need to be productive and prosper?

Neuroscience offers us hope. We know our brains will continue to reconfigure throughout our lives based on our experiences. We can make healthy body and brain choices. We can quell the frenzy, if we will. It is in our power to put the odds in our favor. We can redefine success—for ourselves, for our children. Neuroscience can inform us, helping us to ignite our children's brain development. The choices you make today will help your teen attend the right college and will shape the options he or she has in the future. If everyone else seems to be making other choices, trust your instincts. Trust neuroscience. The emperor has no clothes. It just takes one voice telling the truth to give others better perspective. You know your teen. You know the truth: *genes load the gun; experience pulls the trigger.*

If you feel like you're playing with live wires, you are. Your teenager's crackling brain is high voltage, modern life zaps your energy and your support systems, and everyone's plugged into digital devices 24/7. But you can insulate your family from these powerful forces. Your child is about to leave the nest. If the nest has provided rest, good nutrition, responsive relationships, mentoring, and encouragement, your teen will soar.

ACKNOWLEDGEMENTS

My hearty and deep thanks go to Todd Rose, my colleague and friend who invited me to help him teach the new class in Educational Neuroscience at Harvard University's Graduate School of Education. The popularity of the class surprised him and Harvard alike (but not me—I already knew Todd's brilliance, his wit, his engaging way with people, his deep understanding of neuroscience, his insight into this important field and its implications for education). The class exploded in the numbers of students it attracted, carrying a waitlist and, ultimately, landing on President Drew Faust's watch-list. I have remained a Teaching Fellow for Todd through the continuing classes—we now have logged five classes since its inception. Folks want science they can trust, and they have found it in Todd's class.

Thanks, especially to Dr. Gerard Berry, possibly the smartest man I know, who relates so compassionately to children and their families—for including me in his research projects and never losing patience explaining complex scientific concepts about genetics, metabolism and brain function.

This book comes as a synthesis of the extended family of professors at Harvard—Kurt Fischer, Howard Gardner, David Rose, Jack Shonkoff, Chuck Nelson, Joe Blatt, Paul Harris, Terry Tivnan, Tina Grotzer, Robert Kegan, Lee Coffin, in particular—who changed the way I look at learning and relationships forever. I must also acknowledge the impact of the man at Harvard whom I (and a multitude of others!) consider the penultimate college admission officer: William Fitzsimmons, my first mentor in the college admissions process over twenty-five years ago, whose advice, encouragement, perspective, and friendship over the years have kept me grounded and whole in this industry. My personal thanks to each of you.

To Eliza, thank you for showing me the power of gracious perseverance and reminding me that our inspiration comes from above. To Laura and Tom, my deep appreciation: your understanding of this message has been profoundly meaningful to me.

I must also thank Rob, my husband, for his enormous patience. Not only did I shock him when I told him I had applied and been accepted to yet another graduate program—this time at Harvard—but then when we had just moved my multitudinous stacks of books (and all those shoes!) back to Houston, I mentioned that I would like to commute to Cambridge each Tuesday to help Todd teach his popular and important new class. I believed in Todd; I knew the information gleaned from this class would change lives and could catapult children's learning. Education is at the cusp of change with the information explosion and transformative technology. I simply felt compelled to be a foot soldier in this battle to change the face of education. I needed Rob's support to make this mission possible. He gave it to me without hesitation, and I thank him from the bottom of my heart.

I also thank my children—Chad, Katrin, Lara—and their spouses—Dee, Matthew, Christopher and my nephew Kristopher and his wife Amber. They provided fodder for my investigation and, ultimately, became my own levers that changed my paradigm of how relationships develop over time and how families thrust their genes onto the next generation and pass along their values, traditions, and love. They have given us our precious grandchildren—Grace, Watt, Hale, Prescott, Paysan, Lochlan, Walker, Ebby and grandnephews—Chase and Luke—who have connected us to life, to our souls. I send to each of them abundant family love and hugs of joy. Each has touched us, my husband and me. We have grown along with them. We are grateful. I thank them for their suggestions along the way, their encouragement, their willingness for me to share family moments with others, their reading of drafts, their remembering with kindness some of the moments I might like to have forgotten!

We all live in communities that shape us. Mine is broad and deep. My brother and his wife, my sister-in-law and her husband, my aunts and uncles, my cousins scattered around the country—we have all learned together and shared: family recipes, family stories, family characters.

Though geography separates us, we stand together at the important moments of family crisis and personal need. I am grateful for each one of them and the details that unite us.

Lucy Chambers, my enormously talented editor, and Ellen Cregan, my creative director extraordinaire, have been remarkable thinking partners for this project. I thank them for their encouragement, support, direction, friendship and patience—especially when my first draft fizzled along with my hard drive. Alas, I will always back-up my work in the future! Throughout the process of telling this story, they have been there with just the right words to keep me going. Lucy's pen and Ellen's paintbrush have enriched my message and helped me bring more clarity to each draft. They are the *bright* in their Bright Sky Press—*Where Texas Meets Books*.

Sometimes thank you is simply not enough, but it is a place to begin!

JUDITH WIDENER MUIR has over thirty years of experience in the educational field. As an Independent Educational Consultant, she works with college-bound students throughout the world. Muir has worked with several respected independent schools in the Houston area, including The Kinkaid School. Muir holds her Ed.M. from Harvard University's interdisciplinary Mind, Brain and Education program, which investigates cognitive development, genetics and neuroscience from infancy through early adulthood and their relationship to learning and education. Muir combines her knowledge of education and neuroscience in her theories of neuro-parenting. She uses innovative techniques to help parents and students achieve their educational goals while maintaining healthy, meaningful lives. A Teaching Fellow at Graduate School of Education at Harvard University, Muir and her husband Rob live in Houston, Texas, and have three children and eight grandchildren.

....

GERARD T. BERRY, M.D. is the Harvey Levy Chair in Metabolism and Director of the Metabolism Program at Boston Children's Hospital, Professor of Pediatrics at the Harvard Medical School, and Director of the Harvard Medical School Biochemical Genetics Training Program. Dr. Berry—a biochemical geneticist who works with infants, children and adults with inherited metabolic disorders—is one of the world's leading experts in the study and treatment of galactosemia. He received his Medical Degree from Jefferson Medical College in Philadelphia, then completed his residency in pediatrics at Thomas Jefferson University and a fellowship in biochemical genetics and pediatric endocrinology at the Children's Hospital of Philadelphia/University of Pennsylvania School of Medicine. He is board certified in biochemical genetics, pediatrics and pediatric endocrinology.

NOTES

Chapter Notes

This book is the distillation of a plethora of sources that have filtered through the limestone of my life, so my reference list is rich and full. In order for you to understand the forces that have shaped my perspective, I have included both the books and authors that have informed my work over the years, as well as the studies and scholars that have helped me move from reasonable hypothesis to information grounded in empirical data.

I have written to synthesize and inform, so I am referencing in these notes the sources that have informed my thinking, rather than distracting the message with the footnotes I would have inserted in the text as I do in my academic writing. My readers who want to dig deeper into the research and concepts can use a combination of the text, these notes, and the reference list.

As with many of our ideas and arguments, there comes a point in our life where we cannot always identify the exact source that led us to the threshold of our own minds. I share with you my journey through child development, enriched by my capstone experience at Harvard where—as a grandmother—I put my life on hold and paused to look back over my experiences, professional and personal, motivated by my mother's decline and my grandchildren's emergence, to test my theories and figure out which ones to hold onto and which ones to discard. I write in the hope that you, too, may experience a paradigm shift in how you look at your children, your students, your relationships, your fast-paced life.

CHAPTER ONE: YOUR GENES DO NOT HAVE TO BE YOUR DESTINY

Dr. Gerard Berry, Dr. Charles Nelson, and Dr. Jack Shonkoff, all three pediatricians, each a strong voice for how environmental influences can alter outcome either for good or bad due to remarkable brain plasticity, were among the scholars who garnered my rapt attention during my graduate study. This chapter is based on the paradigm shift I experienced as I heard their presentations, studied their research, talked with them to stretch my own perspective, and then reflected on how their concepts crossed demographic lines. Their rich findings are listed in the Reference section. I began unpacking the new science of epigenetics, looking for clues about how genes can ignite—or not—often depending on environment. The following research, in particular, grounded the message of this chapter:

Berry, G. (2012). Galactosemia: When is it a newborn screening emergency? Mol Genet Metab. 106(1). pp.7-11.

Meaney, M. (2010). Epigenetics and the biological definition of gene x environment interactions. Child Development, 81(1). pp. 41–79.

National Scientific Council on the Developing Child (2010). *Early experiences can alter gene expression and affect long-term development.* Working Paper No. 10.

Shonkoff, J. and Phillips, D. (Eds.). 2000. *From neurons to neighborhoods: The Science of early childhood development.* National Research Council and Institute of Medicine. Washington, D.C.: National Academy Press. pp. 3-56.

Szyf, M. (2009a). Early life, the epigenome and human health. Acta Paediatrica, 98(7). pp. 1082-1084.

Szyf, M. (2009b). The early life environment and the epigenome. Biochimica Biophysica Acta (BBA), 1790(9). pp. 878-885.

Dr. Francis Collins, director of the National Institutes of Health (NIH) and former director of the National Human Genome Research Institute (NHGRI) caught my attention when he said, "Genetics loads the gun and environment pulls the trigger." Curious readers should dig into this article about the important difference between predictive and deterministic and the motivational value of using personal genetic testing to make smarter health choices. Informative article!

Collins, F. (2010). Genetics loads the gun and environment pulls the trigger. http://blog.pathway.com/genetics-loads-the-gun-and-environment-pulls-the-trigger-dr-francis-collins/

CHAPTER TWO: BRAIN BASICS

Much of this chapter is based on John Medina's research and his zingy way of relating it on his website and in his book *Brain Rules.*

Medina, J. (2008). Brain rules. Seattle, WA: Pear Press. pp. 29-70.

David Eagleman introduced me to the concept of neural lightning storms and lightning-fast circuits in our brains. I suggest reading his provocative book *Incognito* to understand better how the brain automates and ties new experiences to past events in the name of efficiency.

Eagleman, D. (2011). Incognito: The secret lives of the brain. New York: Pantheon Books. pp. 1-225.

Conversations with Dr. T. Barry Brazleton reminded me of how much insight he has in what shapes the behaviors of children and drew me back to his research and his books, in particular:

Brazelton, T. B. and Greenspan, S. (2000). The irreducible needs of children: What every child must have to grow, learn, and flourish. Cambridge, MA: Perseus Books. pp. 1-201.

Data confirming the role of relationships to enrich genetic flourish and to mitigate toxic stress is found in The Working Papers from the National Scientific Council on the Developing Child (NSCDC) from Harvard University, which became a catalyst for the messages in this chapter. They are listed in the Reference section and worthy of study for those who are ready to dig into the science that informs us about the architecture of the developing brain. Particularly information for this chapter are the following:

National Scientific Council on the Developing Child (2004). Children's emotional development is built into the architecture of their brains. Working Paper No. 2.

National Scientific Council on the Developing Child (2010). Early experiences can alter gene expression and affect long-term development. Working Paper No. 10.

National Scientific Council on the Developing Child (2005). Excessive stress disrupts the architecture of the developing brain. Working Paper No. 3.
National Scientific Council on the Developing Child. (2007). The Science of Early Childhood Development: Closing the Gap Between What We Know and What We Do.

Shonkoff, J. and Phillips, D. (Eds.). 2000. From neurons to neighborhoods: The Science of early childhood development. National Research Council and Institute of Medicine. Washington, D.C.: National Academy Press. pp. 93-123 and 225-266.

References about the hours students are engaging with media are from the findings of Jane McGonigal and her surprising accounts of what we are learning about the media, a worthy read:

McGonigal, J. (2011). Reality is broken: Why games make us better and how they can change the world. New York: The Penguin Press. pp. 1-354.

CHAPTER THREE: THE AMAZING TEEN BRAIN

As director of a high-powered senior internship program, I have gathered student intern comments over the past twenty-five years. These statements from past seniors inspired me to share my experience with these awesome teens and their observations about their internships. Their insights filled me with awe, and they became the inspiration for this part of the story.

just-in-time learning: David Eagleman (Incognito, p. 71) refers to "flexibility of learning... as fashioning neural circuits to the tasks at hand," much of what an intern must do with a mentor to maximize their learning and stay engaged in the process, essentially "rewiring to accomplish a task with maximum efficiency."

active learning: Mazur, E. (2012). The twilight of the lecture. Harvard Magazine. Retrieved from: http://harvardmagazine.com/2012/03/twilight-of-the-lecture

I found in the writings of Robert Sylwester, a professor and writer who works with teens, who shares my own perspective about "guiding instead of controlling" teens, a lesson I have used over the years in working with my senior interns, as well as his insight about "creative vs rebellious"—after all, novelty-seeking is merely a negative take on creative! Sylwester also references how the brain develops "sequentially, but not simultaneously"—an insightful observation, reflected and substantiated in the research I have done in the Working Papers from the Scientific Council on the Developing Child. I particularly appreciate his perspective that puts teen behavior in the context of cultural expectations—"how-to-do" matures before "whether-to-do"—a point of potential conflict that we as adults can sometimes forget to take into account as we interpret teen responses. Several of the ideas in this chapter are reflections of Sylwester's astute comments about teens in his insightful book:

Sylwester, R. (2007). The adolescent brain reaching for autommy. Thousand Oaks, CA: Corwin Press. pp.1-41 and 81-129.

. . . .

Throughout my book I refer to Mary Carskadon's prolific research at Brown University on adolescent sleep patterns and the price of sleep deprivation on health and productivity. Her research is listed in the Reference section.

. . . .

The role of emotion in learning runs through recent neuroscience research, led by voices like Mary Helen Immordino-Yang and Antonio Damasio. References about emotion are grounded in their works, as well as those of several other scholars, as cited in the Reference section.

Immordino-Yang, M., McColl, A., Damasio, A. & Damasio, H. (2009). Neural correlates of admiration and compassion. *Proceedings of the national academy of sciences*, 106(19). pp. 8021-8026.

internships at seven, not at twenty-seven and *practice forces development*: Gopnik, A. (2012). What's wrong with the teenage mind? *Wall Street Journal*. January 28, Section C, p. 1.

. . . .

porsche engine with model T brakes— from deep and provocative research from Ronald Dahl:

Dahl, R. (2004a). Adolescent development and the regulation of behavior and emotion: Introduction to part VIII. *Annals of the New York Academy of Sciences, 1021*(1). pp. 294-295.

Dahl, R. (2004b). Adolescent brain development: A period of vulnerabilities and opportunities. Keynote address. *Annals of the New York Academy of Sciences, 1021*(1). pp. 1-22.

Dahl, R., and Spear, L. (2004). *Adolescent brain development: Vulnerabilities and opportunities*. New York: New York Academy of Sciences.

teen drivers—several articles in the literature mentioned in Reference section: Chen, L., Baker, S., Braver, E., & Guohua, L. (2000). Carrying passengers as a risk factor for crashes fatal to 16-17 year old drivers. *Journal of the American Medical Assoication, 283*(12). pp.1578-1582. Giedd J. (2005). *Root causes of teen driving accidents, II*, The Allstate Foundation State of Teen Driving Report. http://media. allstate.com/releases/4206-new-research-on-teen.

peer pressure: Blakemore, S., den Ouden, H., Choudhury, S., & Frith, C. (2007). Adolescent development of the nerual circuitry for thinking about intentions. *SCAN, 2*. pp.130-139.

popped out of young minds and *shift from trying to control to trying to mentor*: Sylwester, R. (2007). The adolescent brain reaching for automomy. Thousand Oaks, CA: Corwin Press. pp.1-41 and 81-129.

. . . .

Zone of Proximal Development: Vygotsky, L. (1978). Mind and society: The development of higher psychological processes. Cambridge, MA: MIT Press.

Vygotsky, L. (1986). Thought and language. Cambridge, MA: MIT Press. pp. 190-208.

. . . .

teachers everywhere through the web: Richardson, W. (2010). Blogs, wikis, podcasts, and other powerful web tools for classrooms. Thousand Oaks, CA: Corwin. pp. 1-160.

Richardson, W. and Mancabelli, R. (2011). Personal learning networks: Using the power of connections to transform education. Bloomington, IN: Solution Tree Press. pp. 1-142.

. . . .

second proliferation of neural growth during the teen years: Weinberger, D., Elvevag, B. & Giedd, J. (2005). The adolescent brain: A work in progress. The National Campaign to Prevent Teen Pregnancy. TEENPREGNANCY.org

. . . .

Giedd J., Blumenthal, J., Jeffries, N., Castellanos, F., Liu H., Zijdenbos, A., et al.

(1999). Brain development during childhood and adolescence: A longitudinal MRI study. *Nature Neuroscience, 2*. pp. 861-863.

Giedd, J. (2004). Structural magnetic resonance imaging of the adolescent brain. *Annals of the New York Academy of Sciences, 1021*(1). pp. 77-85.

. . . .

brain plasticity can pattern addictive behaviors: Thompson, R. and Nelson, C. (2001). Developmental science and the media. American Psychologist, 56(1). pp. 5-15.

. . . .

experience gets into our biology: National Scientific Council on the Developing Child (2010). *Early experiences can alter gene expression and affect long-term development*. Working Paper No. 10.

. . . .

Howard Gardner, my advisor in my graduate program at Harvard, has written extensively about intelligence and the many forms it takes. My ideas here branch off of his perspective and keep going from there. Gardner, H. (2000). Intelligence reframed: Multiple intelligences for the 21st century. New York: Basic Books.

CHAPTER FOUR: HEALTHY BRAIN DEVELOPMENT

This chapter draws heavily on Shonkoff and Phillips' *From Neurons to Neighborhoods: The Science of Early Childhood Development*, a book I highly encourage motivated readers to tackle to appreciate the importance of a solid foundation for future good health and cognitive development. Pages 182-212 are of particular interest regarding cell growth;

pruning; brain plasticity; how timing and early experience shape brain development; and how earlier is better than later, but it is never to late for the brain to make adjustments.

Shonkoff, J. and Phillips, D. (Eds.). (2000). From neurons to neighborhoods: The Science of early childhood development. National Research Council and Institute of Medicine. Washington, D.C.: National Academy Press. pp. 182-212.

Dr. Charles Nelson explains the importance of cell migration, pruning, and myelination. Nelson's extensive work with Romanian orphans, research worth digging into for those who want more evidence of the impact of early experience on future healthy development, is widely read and highly respected, though not referenced in the text of *Live Wires*.

Nelson, C. (2004). Brain development during puberty and adolescence: Comments on part II. *Annals of the New York Academy of Sciences, 1021*(1). pp. 105-109.

Nelson, C., Thomas, K., & DeHaan, M. (2006). Neural bases of cognitive development. In D. Kuhn & R.S. Siegler (Eds.), *Handbook of child psychology*, 6th edition, volume 2, chapter 16. Hoboken, N.J.: John Wiley & Sons. pp. 3-19 and 35-39.

Nelson, C., Furtado, E., Fox, A., & Zeanah, C. (2009). The deprived human brain. *American Scientist*, 97, 222-229. http://www.americanscientist.org/issues/id.6380,y.2009,no.3,content.true,page.4,css.print/issue.aspx

Thompson, R. and Nelson, C. (2001). Developmental science and the media. *American Psychologist*, 56(1). pp. 5-15.

Cell growth, communication, neurotransmitter sections in this chapter are also based on explanations in the following text: Banich, M. (2004). Cognitive neuroschience and neuropsychology. Boston: Houghton Mifflin. pp. 3-61 and 285-428.

sensitive and critical periods, especially pruning of circuits not activated by experience: Knudsen, E. (2004). Sensitive periods in the development of the brain and behavior. *Journal of Cognitive Neuroscience*, 16. pp. 1412-1425.

drug interventions can block the reabsorption of chemicals: McEwen, B., and Lasley, E. (2002). The end of stress as we know it. New York: Dana Press. pp. 1-202.

brain plasticity, working around maladapted circuits is harder and riskier: Fischer, K, Ayoub, C., Noam, G., Singh, I., Maraganore, A., & Raya, P. (1997). Psychopathology as adaptive development along distinctive pathways. *Development and Psychopathology*, 9. pp. 751-781.

This chapter also taps into my background reading of the deep research from the National Scientific Council on the Developing Child, which informs the work of Harvard University's Center on the Developing Child, for which Dr. Jack Shonkoff is the Director.

CHAPTER FIVE: DON'T STRESS ME OUT

Bruce McEwen's research on the negative impact of prolonged stress has made me rethink my own lifestyle—and that of my family. I draw extensively on his findings and would direct readers who want to go even further behind the science of stress to his book and studies:

McEwen, B., and Lasley, E. (2002). The end of stress as we know it. New York: Dana Press. pp. 1-202.

McEwen, B. (2008). Central effects of stress hormones in health and disease: Understanding the protective and damaging effects of stress and stress mediators. *European Journal of Pharmacology*, 583. pp. 174-185.

McEwen B. (2012). The ever-changing brain: Cellular and molecular mechanisms for the effects of stressful experiences. Developmental Neurobiology. 72(6). pp. 878-890.

Eiland L. and McEwen B. (2012). Early life stress followed by subsequent adult chronic stress potentiates anxiety and blunts hippocampal structural remodeling. 8, Hippocampus, 22(1). pp. 82-91

....

the stress response can cause damage and accelerate disease: Medina, J. (2008). Brain rules. Seattle, WA: Pear Press. pp. 169-195 and McEwen, B., and Lasley, E. (2002). The end of stress as we know it. New York: Dana Press. pp. 4-5 and Sapolsky, R., Romero, L., & Munck, A. (2000). How do glucorticoids influence stress responses? Integrating permissive, suppressive, stimulatory and preparative actions. *Endocrine Reviews*, 21(1), pp. 55-89.

....

positive stress, tolerable stress, toxic stress (definitions): National Scientific Council on the Developing Child (2005). *Excessive stress disrupts the architecture of the developing brain.* Working Paper No. 3. p. 1.

....

negative physical impact of stress: Society for Neuroscience. (2006). Brain facts: A primer on the brain and nervous system. *Sleep. Stress.* Canada. pp. 4-60 and Gunnar, M. & Davis, E. (2003). Stress and emotion in early childhood. In R.M. Lerner & M.A. Easterbrooks (Eds.), Handbook of Psychology, Vol. 6. Developmental Psychology. New York: Wiley. pp. 113-134.

....

homeostasis and *allostasis* and *the stress response system*: McEwen, B., and Lasley, E. (2002). The end of stress as we know it. New York: Dana Press. pp. 5-16.

....

when a system designed to protect... turn(s) on our body: McEwen, B., and Lasley, E. (2002). The end of stress as we know it. New York: Dana Press. pp. 55-66 and Sapolsky, R., Romero, L., & Munck, A. (2000). How do glucorticoids influence stress responses? Integrating permissive, suppressive, stimulatory and preparative actions. *Endocrine Reviews*, 21(1), pp. 55-89.

....

how does stress cause cardiovascular disease: McEwen, B., and Lasley, E. (2002). The end of stress as we know it. New York: Dana Press. pp. 67-88.

....

stress can ravage parts of your immune system: : McEwen, B., and Lasley, E. (2002). The end of stress as we know it. New York: Dana Press. pp. 89-106 and Medina, J. (2008). Brain rules. Seattle, WA: Pear Press. pp. 169-195.

hippocampus, the seat of memory, responds to stress signals: Weaver, I., Diorio, J., Seckl, J., Szyf, M., & Meaney, M. (2004) Early environmental regulation of hippocampal glucocorticoid receptor gene expression: Characterization of intracellular mediators and potential genomic target sites. Annals of the New York Academy of Sciences, 1024. pp. 182-212 and McEwen, B., and Lasley, E. (2002). The end of stress as we know it. New York: Dana Press. pp. 107-134.

Brain Derived Neurotrophic Factor: McEwen, B., and Lasley, E. (2002). The end of stress as we know it. New York: Dana Press. pp. 161-162, 163,164,168 and Medina, J. (2008). Brain rules. Seattle, WA: Pear Press. pp. 178-180.

exercise produces the magical BDNF: Ratey, J. and Hagerman, E. (2008). Spark: The revolutionary new science of exercise and the brain. New York: Little Brown and Company. pp. 1-268 and McEwen, B., and Lasley, E. (2002). The end of stress as we know it. New York: Dana Press. pp. 161-162, 163,164,168 and Medina, J. (2008). Brain rules. Seattle, WA: Pear Press. pp. 178-180.

buffers to stress (for children)...protective relationship with supportive adult: National Scientific Council on the Developing Child (2005). *Excessive stress disrupts the architecture of the developing brain.* Working Paper No. 3. pp. 2-3.

McEwen and Medina describe how stress upsets balance and then offer guidance about prioritizing lifestyles to restore harmony to your life, as do Hallowell and Keagan. Tony Schwartz also offers constructive ideas about managing stress; I have shared several of his suggestions and perceptions in this chapter with my readers in hopes of helping them shift to a healthier brain and body lifestyle.

interaction between the world we choose to live in and our physiological capacity to manage it: McEwen, B., and Lasley, E. (2002). The end of stress as we know it. New York: Dana Press. pp. 135-172 and Medina, J. (2008). Brain rules. Seattle, WA: Pear Press. pp. 7-28.

stressors are on the rise: McEwen, B., and Lasley, E. (2002). The end of stress as we know it. New York: Dana Press. pp. 16-17.

Hallowell, E. (2006). Crazy Busy: Overstretched, overbooked, and about to snap. NY: Ballentine Books. pp. 1-229.

Hallowell, E. (1997). Worry: Controlling it and using it wisely. New York: Pantheon Books. pp. 1-306.

Kegan, R. & Lahey, L. (2001). How the way we talk can change the way we work. San Francisco, CA: Jossey-Bass. Pp. 1-227.

Kegan, R. & Lahey, L. (2009). Immunity to change: How to overcome it and unlock the potential in yourself and your organization. Boston: Harvard Business Press. pp. 1-64.

as a species, we seek balance and *HPA axis*: McEwen, B., and Lasley, E. (2002). The end of stress as we know it. New York: Dana Press. pp. 135, 140-141, 143, 144.

we take our capacity for granted and *mimic our electronic devices* and *what is the story you tell yourself* and *when demand exceeds capacity*: Schwartz, T. (2010). Be excellent at anything: The four keys to transforming the way we work and live. NY: Free Press. pp. 3-32.

Ratey, J. (2001). A user's guide to the brain. New York: Pantheon Books. pp. 1-378.

Restak, R. (2003). The new brain: How the modern age is rewiring your mind. New York: Rodale Press.

Sapolsky, R. (2004). Why zebras don't have ulcers: An updated guide to stress, stress related diseases, and coping (3rd ed.). New York: Owl Books.

Optimism: Seligman, M. with Reivich, K., Jaycox, L. and Gillham, J. (1995). The optimistic child: A proven program to safeguard children against depression and build lifelong resilience. New York: Houghton Mifflin. pp. 1-305.

Society for Neuroscience. (2006). Brain facts: A primer on the brain and nervous system. *Sleep. Stress.* Canada. pp. 4-60.

CHAPTER SIX: THE HIDDEN COST OF SLEEP DEBT

William Dement, considered by many to be the father of sleep studies, led me to a paradigm shift in recognizing the value of a good night's sleep. Couple his research with that of Mary Carskadon at Brown Univesity, and you will see that America is losing sleep—to its detriment. Readers can delve into their research in the Reference section to see the data

behind the clarion call to get more sleep. Reference to teen sleep deprivation in this chapter pulls heavily on the research of Mary Carskadon and Ronald Dahl, both detailed in the Reference section.

Dement, W. and Carskadon, M. (1982) Current perspectives on daytime sleepiness: The issues. *Sleep* 5: pp. S56-S66.

Dement, W. and Carskadon, M. (1983). Daytime drowsiness: When it indicates a clinically significant problem. *Consultant* 23. pp. 182-199.

Dement, W. and Vaughan, C. (1999). The promise of sleep: A pioneer in sleep medicine explores the vital connection between health, happiness, and a good night's sleep. NY: Dell.

Explanations about what happens during sleep are based on John Medina's accounts from his research in his book *Brain Rules*, listed in the References; readers can go deeper into his research in his book and on his website: Medina, J. (2008). Brain rules. Seattle, WA: Pear Press. pp. 149-168.

if thirty year olds are sleep deprived: Medina, J. (2008). Brain rules. Seattle, WA: Pear Press. pp. 162-163.

if an A student gets under seven hours of sleep and *soldiers drop in...efficiency:* Medina, J. (2008). Brain rules. Seattle, WA: Pear Press. pp. 162.

Carskadon, M., Harvey, K., Duke, P., Anders, T., Litt, I., & Dement, W. (1980). Pubertal changes in daytime sleepiness. *Sleep* 2: pp. 453-460.

Carskadon, M., Acebo, C., & Jenni, O. (2004). Regulation of adolescent sleep: Implications for behavior. *Ann. N.Y. Acad. Sci.* 1021: pp. 276-291.

. . . .

hinders bodies ability to use food: Medina, J. (2008). Brain rules. Seattle, WA: Pear Press. p. 162 and Schwartz, T. (2010). Be excellent at anything: The four keys to transforming the way we work and live. NY: Free Press. p. 60 .

. . . .

sleep deprivation hits the hippocampus: Medina, J. (2008). Brain rules. Seattle, WA: Pear Press. p. 163 and McEwen, B., and Lasley, E. (2002). The end of stress as we know it. New York: Dana Press. p. 142.

. . . .

bricks in the backpack: a concept discussed among students in the graduate class I help teach to develop a metaphor that would help understand the burden of sleep debt

. . . .

Circadian rhythm: McEwen, B., and Lasley, E. (2002). The end of stress as we know it. New York: Dana Press. pp. 25, 142, 145 and Schwartz, T. (2010). Be excellent at anything: The four keys to transforming the way we work and live. NY: Free Press. p. 57-65.

. . . .

vulnerable to enemies: Medina, J. (2008). Brain rules. Seattle, WA: Pear Press. p. 153 and McEwen, B., and Lasley, E. (2002). The end of stress as we know it. New York: Dana Press. p. 141-144.

. . . .

what happens during sleep: Medina, J. (2008). Brain rules. Seattle, WA: Pear Press. p. 155-156.

missed sleep is categorically the same as driving drunk: Carskadon, M. (2002). Risks of driving while sleepy in adolescents and young adults. In *Adolescent Sleep Patterns: Biological, Social, and Psychological Influences*, M. Carskadon (Ed.), Cambridge: University Press. pp. 148-158.

. . . .

brains...locked in vicious, biological combat: Dement, W. as explained in Medina, J. (2008). Brain rules. Seattle, WA: Pear Press. p. 152-156.

. . . .

melatonin is a crucial part: Schwartz, T. (2010). Be excellent at anything: The four keys to transforming the way we work and live. NY: Free Press. p. 61.

. . . .

teen sleep patterns: Carskadon, M.A. (2008). Maturation of processes regulating sleep in adolescents. In Marcus, C., Carroll, J., Donnelly, D., and Loughlin, G. (Eds.). *Sleep in Children, Second Edition*. Informa Healthcare USA, New York, pp 95-114.

Carskadon, M., Harvey, K., Duke, P., Anders, T., Litt, I., & Dement, W. (1980). Pubertal changes in daytime sleepiness. *Sleep* 2: pp. 453-460.

Carskadon, M., Acebo, C., & Jenni, O. (2004). Regulation of adolescent sleep: Implications for behavior. *Ann. N.Y. Acad. Sci.* 1021: pp. 276-291.

Carskadon, M. (2009). Sleep, adolescence, and learning. *Frontiers Neuroscience,* 3(3). pp. 470-471.

Carskadon, M. (2005) Sleep and circadian rhythms in children and adolescents: Implications for athletic performance of young people. *Clin Sports Med* 24:

pp. 319-328.
Carskadon, M. (1999). When worlds collide: Adolescent need for sleep versus societal demands. *Phi Delta Kappan*. **80(5)**. pp. 348-349.

Dahl, R. and Carskadon, M. (1995). Sleep and its disorders in adolescence. In *Principles and Practice of Sleep Medicine in the Child,* R.Ferber and M. Kryger (Eds.), W.B. Saunders, Philadelphia. pp. 19-27.

chatter of neurons: Medina, J. (2008). Brain rules. Seattle, WA: Pear Press. p. 163-164.

sleep cycles and sleep disorders: Sleep disorder data is drawn from scientific accounts in the Society for Neuroscience. (2006). Brain facts: A primer on the brain and nervous system. *Sleep. Stress.* Canada. pp. 4-60. These accounts add to the observation that many of our children could be at risk without adequate sleep— as could we adults.

CHAPTER SEVEN: BE HERE NOW
Flawed attachment is a serious problem that can carry over into adult relationships. Understanding the concept can guide new parents to get it right with engaging relationships where children feel safe and get their needs met from an early age forward. The literature is rich with empirical data, and the Reference section is hefty on this very important topic. Paul Harris, Harvard professor of Child Development, provides considerable data on Attachment Theory and is used here as a point of reference.

Chapter Seven gains its momentum and several points of concern from ideas presented in:

Shonkoff, J. and Phillips, D. (Eds.). (2000). From neurons to neighborhoods: The Science of early childhood development. National Research Council and Institute of Medicine. Washington, D.C.: National Academy Press. pp. 1-413.

In addition, the Working Papers from Harvard University's Center on the Developing Child, prepared by The National Scientific Council on the Developing Child, provide current data on development, in particular:

Working Paper # 2 Children's Emotional Development is Built into the Architecture of their Brains
Working Paper #5 The Timing and Quality of Early Experiences Combine to Shape Brain Architecture

Working Paper #10 Early Experiences Can Alter Gene Expression and Affect Long-Term Development

Working Paper #1 Young Children Develop in an Environment of Relationships.

children develop in the context of relationships: Shonkoff, J. and Phillips, D. (Eds.). (2000). From neurons to neighborhoods: The Science of early childhood development. National Research Council and Institute of Medicine. Washington, D.C.: National Academy Press. pp. 225-266.

"serve and return" dialogue: NSCDC, Young Children develop in an Environment of Relationships, Working Paper #1.

Many of the important ideas I cover about attachment were presented in my Child Development class at Harvard with Paul Harris (2007 lectures cited in Reference section) and Harris, P. (1989). *Children and emotion*. Malden, MA: Blackwell Publishers. pp 1-215.

Early attachment and later development can be found in several sources:

Cassidy, J. & Shaver, P. (Eds.) (1999). Handbook of Attachment: Theory, research, and clinical applications. New York: Guilford. pp. 89-111.

Goldberg, S. (1991). Recent developments in attachment theory and research. *Canadian Journal of Psychiatry*, 36. pp. 393-400.

Thompson, R. & Lagattuta, K. (2006). Feeling and understanding: Early emotional development. In K. McCartney & D. Phillips (Eds.), The Blackwell Handbook of Early Childhood Development. Oxford, UK: Blackwell. pp. 317-337.

Zone of Proximal Development: Vygotsky, L. (1978). Mind and society: The development of higher psychological processes. Cambridge, MA: MIT Press.

quality of first relationships will be predictors of future productivity and health: Knudsen, E., Heckman, J., Cameron, J., & Shonkoff, J. (2006). Economic, neurobiological and behavioral perspectives on building america's future workforce. *Proceedings of the National Academy of Sciences, 103*. pp. 10155-10162.

Ecological Systems Theory: Bronfenbrenner, U. (1979). The ecology of human development: Experiments by nature and design. Cambridge: Harvard University Press. pp. 3-42.

who's minding the children: Brazelton, B. and Greenspan, S. (2000). The irreducible needs of children: What every child must have to grow, learn, and flourish. Cambridge, MA: Perseus Books. pp. 1-201

duet of smiles, gestures...that builds the brain...: NSCDC , Working Paper #1

many childcare workers are the lowest paid and least educated: Shonkoff, J. and Phillips, D. (Eds.). (2000). From neurons to neighborhoods: The Science of early childhood development. National Research Council and Institute of Medicine. Washington, D.C.: National Academy Press. pp. 297-327 and Brazelton, B. and Greenspan, S. (2000). The irreducible needs of children: What every child must have to grow, learn, and flourish. Cambridge, MA: Perseus Books. pp. 1-201.

Waldfogel, J. (1999).The impact of the family and medical leave act. Journal of Policy Analysis and Management, 18(2). pp. 281-302.

NICHD Early Child Care Research Network (1996). Characteristics of infant child care: Factors contributing to positive caregiving. Early Childhood Research Quarterly, 11. pp. 296-306.

NICHD Early Child Care Research Network (2000). Characteristics and quality of child care for toddlers and preschoolers. Applied Developmental Science, 4(3). pp. 116-125.

Weiss, C.H. (1995). Nothing as practical as good theory: Exploring theory-based evaluation for comprehensive community initiatives for children and families. In J.P. Connell, A.C. Kubisch, L.B. Schorr, & C.H. Weiss (Eds.), *New approaches to evaluating community initiatives: Concepts, methods and contexts* (pp. 65-92). Washington , DC: The Aspen Institute.

Yoshikawa, H., & Hsueh, J. (2001). Child development and public policy: Toward a dynamic systems perspective. *Child Development, 72*, 1887-1903.

Hart, B. and Risley, T. (1992**).** American Parenting of Language-Learning Children: Persisting Differences in Family-Child

Interactions Observed in Natural Home Environments, *Developmental Psychology,* Vol. 28, No. 6, 1096-1105

Szucs, D. & Goswami, U., (2007). Educational neuroscience: Defining a new discipline for the study of mental representations. *Mind, Brain, and Education, 1*(3). pp. 114-127.

Heckman, J., & Masterov, D. (2007). The productivity argument for investing in young children. T.W. Shultz Award Lecture presented to the Allied Social Sciences Association. *Review of Agricultural Economics, 29*, 446-493.

. . . .

enrolled in every sport/art/enrichment program available: Elkind, D. (1984). All grown up and no place to go: Teenagers in crisis. Reading, MA: Addison-Wesley. pp. 1-216.

Elkind, D. (2007). The power of play: How spontaneous imaginative activities lead to happier, healthier children. Cambridge, MA: Perseus. pp. 1-218.

. . . .

unconditional love and meaningful engagement: Brazelton, B. and Greenspan, S. (2000). The irreducible needs of children: What every child must have to grow, learn, and flourish. Cambridge, MA: Perseus Books. pp. 1-201

. . . .

crazy about you: by Bronfenbrenner as related in NSCDC, Working Paper #1, p. 1.

CHAPTER EIGHT: MEDIA: MANAGING ITS POTENTIAL

So here I am a grandmother who is supporting video games! When did I morph from suspicious to supportive? When Joe Blatt, Senior Lecturer at Harvard and Director of Technology, Innovation and Education, introduced me to John Paul Gee's insight into what video games could teach us about learning, I had to do an about face. Blatt changed the way I viewed, indeed valued, media. I began to see its phenomenal potential for education. Later, when I heard Jane McGonigal speak about the collaborative edge of gamers and how they persist when they fail to meet their goals 80% of the time, yet keep on going, I knew I had to stand up and listen. This chapter synthesizes McGonigal's message about using games for good and Prensky's and Gee's insistence that classrooms could be more like video games. Motivated readers who want more data should go to these three authors' research, as listed in the Reference section.

Gee, J. (2003). What video games have to teach us about learning and literacy. New York: Palgrave Macmillan. pp. 1-212.

McGonigal, J. (2011). Reality is broken: Why games make us better and how they can change the world. New York: The Penguin Press. pp. 1-354.
Prensky, M. (2000). Digital game-based learning. New York: McGraw-Hill.

Prensky, M. (2001a). Digital natives, digital immigrants. *On the Horizon* 9 (5). pp.1-6. http://www.scribd.com/doc/9799/Prensky-Digital-Natives-Digital-Immigrants-Part1. Archived at http://www.webcitation.org/5eBDYI5Uw.

Prensky, M. (2001b). Digital natives, digital immigrants, part 2: Do they really think differently? *On the Horizon* 9 (6). pp. 1-6. http://www.twitchspeed.com/site/Prensky%20-%20Digital%20Natives,%20Digital%20Immigrants%20-%20Part2.htm. Archived at http://www.webcitation.org/5eBDhJB2N.

Prensky, M. (2009). Innovate: Journal of Online Education. "H. Sapiens Digital: From Digital Immigrants and Digital Natives to Digital Wisdom". 5(3).

http://www.innovateonline.info/index.php?view=article&id=705&action=login

Prensky, M. (2006). Don't bother me, mom: I'm learning. New York: Paragon.

. . . .

But first, reading and relationships and resiliency!

a beautiful place to start - and essential reading for every family with small children; all children's books referenced in the text can be found in: Silvey, A. (Ed.). (2002). The essential guide to children's books and their creators. NY: Houghton Mifflin. pp. 1-498.

invaluable for sleuthing out those beautiful stories that stand the test of time and feature the messages we want our children to hear: Trelease, J. (2006). The read-aloud handbook. NY: Penguin Group. pp. 1-318.

. . . .

relationships develop through engagement: Shonkoff, J. and Phillips, D. (Eds.). (2000). From neurons to neighborhoods: The Science of early childhood development. National Research Council and Institute of Medicine. Washington, D.C.: National Academy Press. pp. 225-266.

National Scientific Council on the Developing Child. (2004). *Young children develop in an environment of relationships*. Working Paper No.1. pp. 1-4.

. . . .

patterns of language development: Wolf, M. (2007). Proust and the squid: The story and science of the reading brain. New York: HarperCollins Publishers. pp. 112-133.

. . . .

child-parent talk in families: Hart, B. and Risley, T. (1992**).** American parenting of language-learning children: Persisting differences in family-child interactions observed in natural home environments, *Developmental Psychology*, Vol. 28, No. 6. pp. 1096-1105.

. . . .

digital natives...digital immigrants: Prensky, M. (2001a). Digital natives, digital immigrants. *On the Horizon* 9 (5). pp.1-6.

. . . .

Kaiser Family Studies are confirming the escalating use of media among children and teens: Rideout, V., Roberts, D., and Foehr, U. (2010). *Generation M2: Media in the lives of 8-18 year-olds*. Executive summary. Menlo Park, CA: Henry J. Kaiser Family Foundation.

. . . .

Universal Design for Learning: Rose, D. and Dalton, B. (2009). Learning to read in the digital age. *Mind, Brain, and Education*, 3(2). Pp. 74-83.

Rose, D. and Gavel, J. (2012). Curricular opportunities in the digital age. Students at the center series, Boston: Jobs for the future. Retrieved online from www.

studentsatthecenter.org/papers/curricular-opportunities-digital-age.

Rose, D. and Meyer, A. (2002). Teaching every student in the digital age: Universal design for learning. Alexandria, VA: Association for Supervision and Curriculum Development. pp. 1-174.

natural variability among our children: Rose, L. T. & Fischer, K. W. (2009). Dynamic systems theory. In R.A. Shweder (Ed.), *Chicago Companion to the Child*. Chicago: University of Chicago Press. pp. 1-6.

negative encounters: Seligman, M. with Reivich, K., Jaycox, L. and Gillham, J. (1995). The optimistic child: A proven program to safeguard children against depression and build lifelong resilience. New York: Houghton Mifflin. pp. 1-305.

average teen has logged...more media... this secondary parallel education: McGonigal, J. (2011). Reality is broken: Why games make us better and how they can change the world. New York: The Penguin Press. pp. 1-354.

harness games for good: McGonigal, J. (2011). Reality is broken: Why games make us better and how they can change the world. New York: The Penguin Press. p 9.

large scale collaboration: McGonigal, J. (2011). Reality is broken: Why games make us better and how they can change the world. New York: The Penguin Press. pp. 13-15, 30-31,75-76, 266-295, 343-344.

a way of thinking, a way of working together to accomplish real change, a platform to enable the future: McGonigal, J. (2011). Reality is broken: Why games make us better and how they can change the world. New York: The Penguin Press. p. 13.

optimism...to conquer learned helplessness: Seligman, M. with Reivich, K., Jaycox, L. and Gillham, J. (1995). The optimistic child: A proven program to safeguard children against depression and build lifelong resilience. New York: Houghton Mifflin. pp. 1-305.

growth mindset: Dweck, C. (2002). The development of ability conceptions. In A. Wigfield & J.S. Eccles (Eds.), *Development of achievement motivation*. San Diego, CA: Academic Press. pp. 57-88 and Dweck, C. (2006). Mindset: The new psychology of success. NY: Random House. pp. 1-239.

flow, optimal experience: Csikszentmihalyi, M. (1990). Flow: The psychology of optimal experience. New York: HarperCollins and as described in McGonigal, J. (2011). Reality is broken: Why games make us better and how they can change the world. New York: The Penguin Press. pp. 24, 35-38, 40-43, 114, 235, 249.

elevated levels of oxytocin and *positive stress*: McGonigal, J. (2011). Reality is broken: Why games make us better and how they can change the world. New York: The Penguin Press. pp. 48, 205, 288 and pp. 32, 62,130-131.

schools should work more like games: McGonigal, J. (2011). Reality is broken: Why games make us better and how they can change the world. New York: The Penguin Press. p. 127-132.

. . . .

challenge of protein folds: McGonigal, J. (2011). Reality is broken: Why games make us better and how they can change the world. New York: The Penguin Press. pp. 236-242.

. . . .

ideas expressed in this section are based on research addressing how electronic media has altered the way children perceive their world, modified the roles of teachers, delivered children to advertisers, immersed children in overconsumption—all issues that beg caution: Singer, D. and Singer, J. (Eds.). (2001). Handbook of children and the media. Thousand Oaks, CA: Sage Publications.

. . . .

children turned over to advertisers: Kunkel, D. (2001). Children and television advertising. Chapter 19 in Singer and Singer and Lamb, S., and L. M. Brown (2007). See no evil? What girls watch. Chapter 2 in *Packaging girlhood: Rescuing our daughters from marketers' schemes*. New York: St. Martin's Griffin.

. . . .

some positive educational components: Schmidt, M., and Anderson, D. (2006). The impact of television on cognitive development and educational achievement. In N. Pecora, J. P. Murray, and E. A. Wartella, (Eds.). *Children and television: Fifty years of research*. Mahwah, NJ: Lawrence Erlbaum Associates and Smith, S., Smith, S., Pieper, K., Yoo, K., Ferris, A., Downs, E and Bowden, B. (2006). Altruism on American television: Examining the amount of, and context surrounding, acts of helping and sharing. *Journal of Communication, 56*, pp. 707-727.

. . . .

tools which foster learning: Anderson, D. (2004). Watching children watch television and the creation of *blue's clues*. In H. Hendershot (Ed.). *Nickelodeon nation: The history, politics, and economics of America's only TV channel for kids*. New York: New York University Press and Fisch, S. M., R. T. Truglio, and C. F. Cole (1999). The impact of *Sesame Street* on preschool children: A review and synthesis of 30 years' research. *Media Psychology, 1*, 165-190.

. . . .

theory of conservation: Piaget, J. & Szeminska, A. (1941). The child's conception of number. Selected pages reprinted in Gruber, H.E.& Voneche, J.J. (1977). *The essential Piaget*. New Jersey: Jason Aronson Inc. pp. 298-311 and Piaget, J. (1952[1936]). The origins of intelligence in children. International University Press.

. . . .

mental representations: Szucs, D. & Goswami, U., (2007). Educational neuroscience: Defining a new discipline for the study of mental representations. *Mind, Brain, and Education, 1*(3), pp. 114-127.

. . . .

aggression may be a learned response: Bushman, B. and Huesmann, L. (2001). Effects of televised violence on aggression. Chapter 11 in Singer and Singer and Huesmann, L. (2007). The impact of electronic media violence: Scientific theory and research. *Journal of Adolescent Health*, vol 41, 6, supplement 1.

family viewing habits: Champ, J. (2004). "Couch potatodom" reconsidered: The vogels and the carsons. In S. M. Hoover, L. S. Clark, and D. F. Alters. *Media, home and family*. New York and London: Routledge and Livingstone, S. (2002). Living together separately: The family context of media use. Chapter 5 in *Young people and new media: Childhood and the changing media environment*. Thousand Oaks, CA: Sage Publications

viewing standards: Bandura, A. (2001). Social cognitive theory of mass communication. *Media Psychology, 3*. pp. 265-299

research is challenging to compile: Jordan, A. (1996). *The state of children's television: An examination of quantity, quality, and industry beliefs*. Philadelphia: The Annenberg Public Policy Center of the University of Pennsylvania.

amount of engagement that occurs among family member: Mares, M. and Woodard, E. (2001). Prosocial effects on children's social interactions. Chapter 9 in Singer and Singer.

engagement for genuine learning: Rideout, V., and Hamel, E. (2006). *The media family: Electronic media in the lives of infants, toddlers, preschoolers, and their parents*. Menlo Park, CA: Henry J. Kaiser Family Foundation

CHAPTER NINE: GETTING INTO THE RIGHT COLLEGE

The road to college, while filled with good intentions, can be replete with moments when challenge can morph into threat, potentially setting off a teen's stress response system, potentially throwing an anxious teen—and a family—off balance. To understand our teens, it is important to understand their brains. To fix education and preserve our economy and culture, it is important to understand how learning occurs. We need to think deeply about child-parent communication and the power of words to transmit covert messages and deliver emotional wounds. This chapter takes a hard look at our perceptions, how we got to them, and what we might do to keep our children healthy as they move into adulthood.

Zito, J., Safer, D., dosReis, S., Gardner, J., Boles, M., & Lynch, F. (2000).Trends in the prescribing of psychotropic medications to preschoolers. Journal of the American Medical Association, 283(8). pp. 1025-1030.

vtrigger depression: Seligman, M. with Reivich, K., Jaycox, L. and Gillham, J. (1995). The optimistic child: A proven program to safeguard children against depression and build lifelong resilience. New York: Houghton Mifflin. pp. 1-305.

Acebo, C. and Carskadon, M. (2002). Influence of irregular sleep/wake patterns on waking behavior. In *Adolescent Sleep Patterns: Biological, Social, and Psychological Influences*, M. Carskadon (Ed.), Cambridge: University Press, pp. 220-235.

Carskadon, M.A. (Editor). (2002). *Adolescent Sleep Patterns: Biological, Social, and Psychological Influences*. Cambridge: University Press.

Carskadon, M. (2002). Factors influencing sleep patterns of adolescents. In *Adolescent Sleep Patterns: Biological, Social, and Psychological Influences*, M.A. Carskadon (Ed.), Cambridge: University Press. pp. 4-26.

Carskadon, M.A. (2008). Maturation of processes regulating sleep in adolescents. In Marcus, C., Carroll, J., Donnelly, D., and Loughlin, G. (Eds.). *Sleep in Children, Second Edition*. Informa Healthcare USA, New York, pp 95-114.

Carskadon, M., Harvey, K., Duke, P., Anders, T., Litt, I., & Dement, W. (1980). Pubertal changes in daytime sleepiness. *Sleep* 2: pp. 453-460.

Carskadon, M., Acebo, C., & Jenni, O. (2004). Regulation of adolescent sleep: Implications for behavior. *Ann. N.Y. Acad. Sci.* 1021: pp. 276-291.

Carskadon, M. (2002). Risks of driving while sleepy in adolescents and young adults. In *Adolescent Sleep Patterns: Biological, Social, and Psychological Influences*, M. Carskadon (Ed.), Cambridge: University Press. pp. 148-158.

Carskadon, M. (2009). Sleep, adolescence, and learning. *Frontiers Neuroscience,* 3(3). pp. 470-471.

Carskadon, M. (2005) Sleep and circadian rhythms in children and adolescents: Implications for athletic performance of young people. *Clin Sports Med* 24: pp. 319-328.

Carskadon, M. and Tarokh, L. (2009). Sleep in child and adolescent development. In Klockars, M. and Porkka-Heiskanen, T. (Eds.) *The Many Aspects of Sleep*. Acta Gyllenbergiana VIII. Helsinki: The Signe and Ane Gyllenberg Foundation, pp 89-100.

Carskadon, M. (1999). When worlds collide: Adolescent need for sleep versus šocietal demands. *Phi Delta Kappan.* **80(5)**. pp. 348-349.

McEwen, B. (2008). Central effects of stress hormones in health and disease: Understanding the protective and damaging effects of stress and stress mediators. *European Journal of Pharmacology*, 583, pp. 174-185.

McEwen, B., and Lasley, E. (2002). The end of stress as we know it. New York: Dana Press. pp. 1-202.

Eiland L. and McEwen B. (2012). Early life stress followed by subsequent adult chronic stress potentiates anxiety and blunts hippocampal structural remodeling. 8 HIPPOCAMPUS, 22(1). pp. 82-91.

. . . .

overscheduling: Elkind, D. (1984). All grown up and no place to go: Teenagers in crisis. Reading, MA: Addison-Wesley. pp. 1-216.

Elkind, D. (2007). The power of play: How spontaneous imaginative activities lead to happier, healthier children. Cambridge, MA: Perseus. pp. 1-218.

. . . .

achievement obsessed parents can damage children and deliver mixed messages and *paramilitants*: Weissbourd, R. (2009). The parents we mean to be: How well-intentioned adults undermine children's moral and emotional development. New York: Houghton Mifflin Harcourt Brace Publishing. p. 4 and pp. 1-206.

We learned early in our parenting days from Haim Ginott the destructive power of words and how to be protective of our children's feelings, how to transmit values without demanding compliance. We taught our children to criticize the act, but never to criticize the person. Label the act, not the person. People live up to the labels we give them. Messages between children and parents is often in "code." I still recommend his work:

. . . .

revolutionizing parent-child communication:
Ginott, H. (1965). Between parent and child. NY: Macmillan. Revised and updated by Ginott, A. and Goddard, H. (2003). Between parent and child. NY: Three Rivers Press.

. . . .

emotional problems cross demographic lines: Luthar, S. S. (2006).

"Overscheduling" versus other stressors: Challenges of high socioeconomic status families.Social Policy Report, Society for Research in Child Development.

Luthar, S. S., Shoum, K. A.,Brown, P.J. (2006). Extracurricular involvement among affluent youth: A scapegoat for "ubiquitous achievement pressures"?. Developmental Psychology, 42, 583-597.

Luthar, S. S., & Latendresse, S. J. (2005). Children of the affluent: Challenges to well-being. Current Directions in Psychological Science,14 , 49-53.

Luthar, S. S., & Sexton, C. (2005). The high price of affluence. In R. V. Kail (Ed.), Advances in Child Development, 32, 126-162. San Diego, CA: Academic Press.

Luthar, S. S. (2003). The culture of affluence: Psychological costs of material wealth. Child Development, 74, 1581-1593.

Simpson, A. Rae. (2001). Raising teens: A synthesis of research and a foundation for action. Boston: Center for Health Communication, Harvard School of Public Health. pp. 1-68.

Gould, S. (1996). The mismeasure of man. New York: Norton. pp. 176-263.

Gardner, H. (2000). The disciplined mind: Beyond facts and standardized tests, the K-12 education that every child deserves. NY: Penguin Group.

Gardner, H. (2006). Five minds for the future. Cambridge: Harvard Business School Press.

Gardner, H. (2000). Intelligence reframed: Multiple intelligences for the 21st century. NY: Basic Books.

Gardner, H. (2004). The unschooled mind: How children think and how schools should teach. NY: Basic Books.

Stein, Z., Dawson, T. & Fischer, K. (2010). Redesigning testing: Operationalizing the new science of learning. In Khine &Saleh (Eds.). *The new science of learning: Computers, cognition and collaboration education.* Springer Press

Sternberg, R. (1996). Successful intelligence: How practical and creative intelligence determine success in life. New York: Simon and Schuster.

Sternberg, R. (1997). Thinking Styles. Cambridge: University Press.

Alloway, T. (2006). How does working memory work in the classroom? *Educational Research and Reviews*, 1(4). pp. 134-149.

Weinberger, D., Elvevag, B. & Giedd, J. (2005). The adolescent brain: A work in progress. The National Campaign to Prevent Teen Pregnancy. TEENPREGNANCY.org

References

Acebo, C. and Carskadon, M. (2002). Influence of irregular sleep/wake patterns on waking behavior. In *Adolescent Sleep Patterns: Biological, Social, and Psychological Influences*, M. Carskadon (Ed.), Cambridge: University Press, pp. 220-235.

Alloway, T. (2006). How does working memory work in the classroom? *Educational Research and Reviews*, 1(4). pp. 134-149.

Anderson, D. (2004). Watching children watch television and the creation of *blue's clues*. In H. Hendershot (Ed.). *Nickelodeon nation: The history, politics, and economics of America's only TV channel for kids*. New York: New York University Press.

Ansary, N. A. & Luthar, S. S. (2009). Distress and academic achievement among adolescents of affluence: A study of externalizing and internalizing problem behaviors and school performance. Development and Psychopathology, 21, 319-341.

Bandura, A. (2001). Social cognitive theory of mass communication. *Media Psychology, 3*. pp. 265-299.

Banich, M. (2004). Cognitive neuroschience and neuropsychology. Boston: Houghton Mifflin. pp. 3-61 and 285-428.

Barker, D., Osmond, C., Forsen, T., Kajantie, E., & Erikson, J. (2005). Trajectories of growth among children who have coronary events as adults. *The New England Journal of Medicine, 353,* 1802-1809.

Becker, B., & Luthar S. S. (2007). Peer-perceived admiration and social preference: contextual correlates of positive peer regard among suburban and urban adolescents. Journal of research on adolescence, 17(1), 117-144.

Berry, G. (2012). Galactosemia: When is it a newborn screening emergency? Mol Genet Metab. 106(1). pp.7-11.

Blakemore, S., den Ouden, H., Choudhury, S., & Frith, C. (2007). Adolescent development of the nerual circuitry for thinking about intentions. *SCAN, 2*. pp. 130-139.

Brazelton, T. B. and Greenspan, S. (2000). The irreducible needs of children: What every child must have to grow, learn, and flourish. Cambridge, MA: Perseus Books. pp. 1-201.

Bronfenbrenner, U. (1979). The ecology of human development: Experiments by nature and design. Cambridge: Harvard University Press. pp. 3-42.

Brooks, R. and Goldstein, S. (2003). Nurturing resilience in our children: Answers to the most important parenting questions. New York: McGraw Hill. pp. 1-234.

Bushman, B. and Huesmann, L. (2001). Effects of televised violence on aggression. Chapter 11 in Singer and Singer.

Carr, N. (2008a). Is Google making us stupid? What the internet is doing to our brains. *The Atlantic* 301 (6). pp. 56-63. http://www.theatlantic.com/doc/200807/google. Archived at http://www.webcitation.org/5eBJxMMM3.

Carskadon, M.A. (Editor). (2002). *Adolescent Sleep Patterns: Biological, Social, and Psychological Influences.* Cambridge: University Press.

Carskadon, M. (2002). Factors influencing sleep patterns of adolescents. In *Adolescent Sleep Patterns: Biological, Social, and Psychological Influences*, M.A. Carskadon (Ed.), Cambridge: University Press. pp. 4-26.

Carskadon, M.A. (2008). Maturation of processes regulating sleep in adolescents. In Marcus, C., Carroll, J., Donnelly, D., and Loughlin, G. (Eds.). *Sleep in Children, Second Edition.* Informa Healthcare USA, New York, pp 95-114.

Carskadon, M., Harvey, K., Duke, P., Anders, T., Litt, I., & Dement, W. (1980). Pubertal changes in daytime sleepiness. *Sleep* 2: pp. 453-460.

Carskadon, M., Acebo, C., & Jenni, O. (2004). Regulation of adolescent sleep: Implications for behavior. *Ann. N.Y. Acad. Sci.* 1021: pp. 276-291.

Carskadon, M. (2002). Risks of driving while sleepy in adolescents and young adults. In *Adolescent Sleep Patterns: Biological, Social, and Psychological Influences*, M. Carskadon (Ed.), Cambridge: University Press. pp. 148-158.

Carskadon, M. (2009). Sleep, adolescence, and learning. *Frontiers Neuroscience,* 3(3). pp. 470-471.

Carskadon, M. (2005) Sleep and circadian rhythms in children and adolescents: Implications for athletic performance of young people. *Clin Sports Med* 24: pp. 319-328.

Carskadon, M. and Tarokh, L. (2009). Sleep in child and adolescent development. In Klockars, M. and Porkka-Heiskanen, T. (Eds.) *The Many Aspects of Sleep*. Acta Gyllenbergiana VIII. Helsinki: The Signe and Ane Gyllenberg Foundation, pp 89-100.

Carskadon, M. (1999). When worlds collide: Adolescent need for sleep versus societal demands. *Phi Delta Kappan.* **80(5)**. pp. 348-349.

Cassidy, J. & Shaver, P. (Eds.) (1999). Handbook of Attachment: Theory, research, and clinical applications. New York: Guilford. pp. 89-111.

Champ, J. (2004). "Couch potatodom" reconsidered: The vogels and the carsons. In S. M. Hoover, L. S. Clark, and D. F. Alters. *Media, home and family*. New York and London: Routledge.

Chen, L., Baker, S., Braver, E., & Guohua, L. (2000). Carrying passengers as a risk factor for crashes fatal to 16-17 year old drivers. *Journal of the American Medical Assoication, 283*(12). pp.1578-1582.

Christianson, C., Horn, M. & Johnson, C. (2008). Disrupting class: How disruptive innovation will change the way the world learns. New York: McGraw Hill. pp. 1-230.

Cohn, L., Macfarlane, S., & Yanez, C. (1995). Risk-perception: Differences between adolescents and adults. *Health Psychology, 14*(3). pp. 217-222.

Collins, F. (2010). Genetics loads the gun and environment pulls the trigger. http://blog.pathway.com/genetics-loads-the-gun-and-environment-pulls-the-trigger-dr-francis-collins/.

Csikszentmihalyi, M. (1990). Flow: The psychology of optimal experience. New York: HarperCollins.

Dahl, R. (2004a). Adolescent development and the regulation of behavior and emotion: Introduction to part VIII. *Annals of the New York Academy of Sciences, 1021*(1). pp. 294-295.

Dahl, R. (2004b). Adolescent brain development: A period of vulnerabilities and opportunities. Keynote address. *Annals of the New York Academy of Sciences, 1021*(1). pp. 1-22.

Dahl, R., and Spear, L. (2004). *Adolescent brain development: Vulnerabilities and opportunities*. New York: New York Academy of Sciences.

Dahl, R. and Carskadon, M. (1995). Sleep and its disorders in adolescence. In *Principles and Practice of Sleep Medicine in the Child*, R.Ferber and M. Kryger (Eds.), W.B. Saunders, Philadelphia. pp. 19-27.

Damasio, A. (2003). Looking for Spinoza: Joy, sorrow, and the feeling brain. New York: Harcourt.

Damasio, A. (1999). The feeling of what happens: Body and emotion in the making of consciousness. New York: Harcourt.

Danese, A., Moffitt, T., Harrington, H., Milne, B., Polanczyk, G., Pariante, C., Poulton, R., & Caspi, A. (2009). Adverse childhood experiences and adult risk factors for age-related disease. *Archives of Pediatrics and Adolescent Medicine, 163*, 1135-1143.

Deci, E., Vallerand, R. Pelletier, L., & Ryan, R. (1991). Motivation and education: The self-determination perspective. *Educational Psychologist, 26*(3/4). pp. 325-346.

Dement, W. and Carskadon, M. (1982) Current perspectives on daytime sleepiness: The issues. *Sleep* 5: pp. S56-S66.

Dement, W. and Carskadon, M. (1983). Daytime drowsiness: When it indicates a clinically significant problem. *Consultant* 23. pp. 182-199.

Dement, W. and Vaughan, C. (1999). The promise of sleep: A pioneer in sleep medicine explores the vital connection between health,happiness, and a good night's sleep. NY: Dell.

Dietrich, C. (2010). Decision making: Factors that influence decision making, heuristics used, and decision outcomes. *Student Pulse*, 2.02. Retrieved from: http://www.studentpulse.com/a?id=180.

Dobbs, D. (2009). Orchid children. *The Atlantic December*. pp.60-68. http://www.theatlantic.com/doc/200912/dobbs-orchid-gene

Dweck, C. (2002). The development of ability conceptions. In A. Wigfield & J.S. Eccles (Eds.), *Development of achievement motivation*. San Diego, CA: Academic Press. pp. 57-88.

Dweck, C. (2006). Mindset: The new psychology of success. NY: Random House. pp. 1-239.

Eagleman, D. (2011). Incognito: The secret lives of the brain. New York: Pantheon Books. pp. 1-225.

Eiland L. and McEwen B. (2012). Early life stress followed by subsequent adult chronic stress potentiates anxiety and blunts hippocampal structural remodeling. 8 HIPPOCAMPUS, 22(1). pp. 82-91.

Elkind, D. (1984). All grown up and no place to go: Teenagers in crisis. Reading, MA: Addison-Wesley. Pp. 1-216.

Elkind, D. (2007). The power of play: How spontaneous imaginative activities lead to happier, healthier children. Cambridge, MA: Perseus. pp. 1-218.

Engle, P., Black, M., Behrman, J., Cabral de Mello, M., Gertler, P., Kapiriri, L., Martorell, R., Young, M., & the International Child Development Steering Group. (2007). Strategies to avoid the loss of developmental potential in more than 200 million children in the developing world. Lancet, 369, 229-242.

Fisch, S. M., R. T. Truglio, and C. F. Cole (1999). The impact of Sesame Street on preschool children: A review and synthesis of 30 years' research. Media Psychology, 1, 165-190.

Fischer, K. (2009). Mind, Brain, and Education: Building a scientific groundwork for learning and teaching. Mind, Brain, and Education, 3. pp. 2-15.

Fischer, K. and Immordino-Yang, M. (2008). The fundamental importance of the brain and learning for education. The Jossey-Bass Reader on the Brain and Learning. San Francisco: Jossey-Bass. xvii-xxi.

Fischer, K., Bernstein, J. & Immordino-Yang, M. (Eds.). (2007). Mind, brain, and education in reading disorders. Cambridge UK: University Press. pp. 181-238.
Fischer, K, Ayoub, C., Noam, G., Singh,

I., Maraganore, A., & Raya, P. (1997). Psychopathology as adaptive development along distinctive pathways. Development and Psychopathology, 9. pp. 751-781.

Galvan, A. (2010). Neural plasticity of development and learning. Human Brain Mapping, 31. pp. 879-890.

Gardner, H. (2004). Changing minds: The art and science of changing our own and other people's minds. Boston: Harvard Business School Press.

Gardner, H. (2000). The disciplined mind: Beyond facts and standardized tests, the K-12 education that every child deserves. NY: Penguin Group.

Gardner, H. (2006). Five minds for the future. Cambridge: Harvard Business School Press.

Gardner, H. (2000). Intelligence reframed: Multiple intelligences for the 21st century. NY: Basic Books.

Gardner, H. (2004). The unschooled mind: How children think and how schools should teach, NY: Basic Books.

Gardner, H., Csikzentmihalyi, M., and Damon, W. (2001). Good work: When excellence and ethics meet. New York: Basic Books.

Gee, J. (2003). What video games have to teach us about learning and literacy. New York: Palgrave Macmillan. pp. 1-212.

Giedd J. (2005). Root causes of teen driving accidents, II, The Allstate Foundation State of Teen Driving Report. http://media.allstate.com/releases/4206-new-research-on-teen.

Giedd J., Blumenthal, J., Jeffries, N., Castellanos, F., Liu H., Zijdenbos, A., et al. (1999). Brain development during childhood and adolescence: A longitudinal MRI study. *Nature Neuroscience, 2*. pp. 861-863.

Giedd, J. (2004). Structural magnetic resonance imaging of the adolescent brain. *Annals of the New York Academy of Sciences, 1021*(1). pp. 77-85.

Ginott, H. (1965). Between parent and child. NY: Macmillan. Revised and updated by Ginott, A. and Goddard, H. (2003). Between parent and child. NY: Three Rivers Press.

Goldberg, S. (1991). Recent developments in attachment theory and research. *Canadian Journal of Psychiatry*, 36. pp. 393-400.

Gopnik, A., Meltzoff, A. & Kuhl, P. (1999). The scientist in the crib: What early learning tells us about the mind. New York: HarperCollins.

Gopnik, A. (2012). What's wrong with the teenage mind? *Wall Street Journal*. January 28, Section C, p. 1.

Gormley, W. (2007). Early childhood care and education: Lessons and puzzles. *Journal of Policy Analysis and Management, 26*, 633-671.

Gould, S. (1996). The mismeasure of man. New York: Norton. pp. 176-263.

Gray, H. (1995). It's a different world where you come from. Chapter 6 in *Watching race: Television and the struggle for "blackness."* Minneapolis: University of Minnesota Press.

Griffin, S., Case, R., Siegler, R. (1994). Rightstart: Providing the central conceptual prerequisites for the first formal learning of arithmetic to students at risk for school failure. In K. McGilly (Ed.), *Classroom lessons: Integrating cognitive theory and classroom practice.* Cambridge, MA: MIT Press. pp. 25-49.

Gunnar, M. & Davis, E. (2003). Stress and emotion in early childhood. In R.M. Lerner & M.A. Easterbrooks (Eds.), Handbook of Psychology, Vol. 6. Developmental Psychology. New York: Wiley. pp. 113-134.

Hallowell, E. (2006). Crazy Busy: Overstretched, overbooked, and about to snap. NY: Ballentine Books. pp. 1-229.

Hallowell, E. (1997). Worry: Controlling it and using it wisely. New York: Pantheon Books. pp. 1-306.

Harris, P. (2007, September 18). Attachment and the effects of early deprivation. [H-250 Lecture, HGSE]. Cambridge, MA.

Harris, P. (2007, October 30). Emotions and understanding emotions. [H-250 Lecture, HGSE]. Cambridge, MA.

Harris, P. (2007, November 1). Emotion and understanding emotions. [H-250 Lecture, HGSE). Cambridge, MA.

Harris, P. (1989). *Children and emotion.* Malden, MA: Blackwell Publishers. pp 1-215.

Harris, P. (in press). Understanding emotion. To appear in M. Lewis & J. M. Haviland-Jones (Eds.) Handbook of Emotions 3rd edition. New York: Guilford Press.

Hart, B. and Risley, T. (1992). American parenting of language-learning children: Persisting differences in family-child interactions observed in natural home environments, *Developmental Psychology*, Vol. 28, No. 6. pp. 1096-1105.

Heckman, J., & Masterov, D. (2007). The productivity argument for investing in young children. T.W. Shultz Award Lecture presented to the Allied Social Sciences Association. *Review of Agricultural Economics, 29*, 446-493.

Hinton, C. and Fischer, K. (2008). Research schools: Grounding research I educational practice. *Mind, Brain, and Education*, 2. pp. 157-160.

Huesmann, L. (2007). The impact of electronic media violence: Scientific theory and research. *Journal of Adolescent Health*, vol 41, 6, supplement 1.

Hofschire, L. and Greenberg, B. (2002). Media's impact on adolescents' body dissatisfaction. In J. D. Brown, J. R. Steele, and K. Walsh-Childers (Eds.). *Sexual teens, sexual media: Investigating media's influence on adolescent sexuality*. Mahwah, NJ: Lawrence Erlbaum Associates.

Horning, K. (1997). From cover to cover: Evaluating and reviewing children's books. NY: Harper Collins. pp. 1-220.

Ilg, F., Ames, L. & Baker, S. (1981). Child Behavior: The classic child care manual from the Gesell Institute of Human Development. New York: HarperCollins. pp. 1-347.

Immordino-Yang, M., McColl, A., Damasio, A. & Damasio, H. (2009). Neural correlates of admiration and compassion. *Proceedings of the national academy of sciences*, 106(19). pp. 8021-8026.

Jenni, O. and Carskadon, M. (Guest Eds.). (2007). *Sleep Medicine Clinics: Sleep in Children and Adolescents*. Philadelphia. W.B. Saunders (Elsevier), Philadephia.

Jordan, A. (1996). *The state of children's television: An examination of quantity, quality, and industry beliefs*. Philadelphia: The Annenberg Public Policy Center of the University of Pennsylvania.

Kegan, R. & Lahey, L. (2001). How the way we talk can change the way we work. San Francisco, CA: Jossey-Bass. Pp. 1-227.

Kegan, R. & Lahey, L. (2009). Immunity to change: How to overcome it and unlock the potential in yourself and your organization. Boston: Harvard Business Press. pp. 1-64.

Kishiyama, M., Boyce, W.T., Jimenez, A., Perry, L., & Knight, R. (2009). Socioeconomic disparities affect prefrontal function in children. *Journal of Cognitive Neuroscience, 21*, 1106-1115.

Kohn, A. (2005). Unconditional parenting: Moving from rewards and punishments to love and reason. New York: Atria Books.

Knudsen, E., Heckman, J., Cameron, J., & Shonkoff, J. (2006). Economic, neurobiological and behavioral perspectives on building america's future workforce. *Proceedings of the National Academy of Sciences, 103*. pp. 10155-10162.

Knudsen, E. (2004). Sensitive periods in the development of the brain and behavior. *Journal of Cognitive Neuroscience, 16*. pp. 1412-1425.

Kunkel, D. (2001). Children and television advertising. Chapter 19 in Singer and Singer.

Lamb, S., and L. M. Brown (2007). See no evil? What girls watch. Chapter 2 in *Packaging girlhood: Rescuing our daughters from marketers' schemes*. New York: St. Martin's Griffin.

LeDoux, J. (2000). Emotion circuits in the brain. Annual Review of Neuroscience, 23,. pp. 155-184.

LeDoux, J. (1996). The emotional brain. NY: Simon & Schuster.

LeDoux, J. (2002). Synaptic self: How our brains become who we are. NY: Penguin.

Livingstone, S. (2002). Living together separately: The family context of media use. Chapter 5 in *Young people and new media: Childhood and the changing media environment*. Thousand Oaks, CA: Sage Publications.

Loehr, J., and Schwartz, T. (2010). The power of full engagement: Managing energy, not time, is the key to high performance and personal renewal. New York: Simon and Schuster. pp. 1-195.

Luthar, S. S. (2006). "Overscheduling" versus other stressors: Challenges of high socioeconomic status families.Social Policy Report, Society for Research in Child Development.

Luthar, S. S., Shoum, K. A.,Brown, P.J. (2006). Extracurricular involvement among affluent youth: A scapegoat for "ubiquitous achievement pressures"?. Developmental Psychology, 42, 583-597.

Luthar, S. S., & Latendresse, S. J. (2005). Children of the affluent: Challenges to well-being. Current Directions in Psychological Science,14 , 49-53.

Luthar, S. S., & Sexton, C. (2005). The high price of affluence. In R. V. Kail (Ed.), Advances in Child Development, 32, 126-162. San Diego, CA: Academic Press.

Luthar, S. S. (2003). The culture of affluence: Psychological costs of material wealth.Child Development, 74, 1581-1593.

Mares, M. and Woodard, E. (2001). Prosocial effects on children's social interactions. Chapter 9 in Singer and Singer.

Mazur, E. (2012). The twilight of the lecture. Harvard Magazine. Retrieved from: http://harvardmagazine.com/2012/03/twilight-of-the-lecture

McEwen, B. (2008). Central effects of stress hormones in health and disease: Understanding the protective and damaging effects of stress and stress mediators. *European Journal of Pharmacology*, 583, pp. 174-185.

McEwen, B., and Lasley, E. (2002). The end of stress as we know it. New York: Dana Press. pp. 1-202.

McEwen B. (2012). The ever-changing brain: Cellular and molecular mechanisms for the effects of stressful experiences. DEV NEUROBIOLOGY. 72(6). pp. 878-890.

McGonigal, J. (2011). Reality is broken: Why games make us better and how they can change the world. New York: The Penguin Press. pp. 1-354.

Meaney, M. (2010). Epigenetics and the biological definition of gene x environment interactions. *Child Development, 81,* 41-79.

Means Coleman, R. (2002). The Menace II society copycat murder case and thug life: A reception study with a convicted criminal. In R. R. Means Coleman (Ed.). *Say it loud! African-american audiences, media and identity.* New York: Routledge.

Medina, J. (2008). Brain rules. Seattle, WA: Pear Press. pp. 1-280.

National Scientific Council on the Developing Child (2011). *Building the brain's "air traffic control" system: How early experiences shape the development of executive function.* Working Paper No. 11.

National Scientific Council on the Developing Child (2004). *Children's emotional development is built into the architecture of their brains.* Working Paper No. 2.

National Scientific Council on the Developing Child (2010). *Early experiences can alter gene expression and affect long-term development.* Working Paper No. 10.

National Scientific Council on the Developing Child (2005). *Excessive stress disrupts the architecture of the developing brain.* Working Paper No. 3.

National Scientific Council on the Developing Child. (2007). *The Science of Early Childhood Development: Closing the Gap Between What We Know and What We Do.* http://developingchild.harvard.edu/ library/reports_and_working_papers/ science_of_early_childhood_development/

National Scientific Council on the Developing Child. (2008). *The timing and quality of early experiences combine to shape brain architecture.* Working Paper No.5

National Scientific Council on the Developing Child. (2004). *Young children develop in an environment of relationships.* Working Paper No.1.

National Scientific Council on the Developing Child. (2010). *Persistent fear and anxiety can affect young children's learning and development.* Working Paper No. 9. http://developingchild.harvard. edu/library/reports_and_working_papers/ working_papers/wp9/

National Television Violence Study (1996). Executive summary, volume 1. Studio City, CA: Mediascope.

Nelson, C. (2004). Brain development during puberty and adolescence: Comments on part II. *Annals of the New York Academy of Sciences, 1021*(1). pp. 105-109.

Nelson, C., Thomas, K., & DeHaan, M. (2006). Neural bases of cognitive development. In D. Kuhn & R.S. Siegler (Eds.), *Handbook of child psychology,* 6th edition, volume 2, chapter 16. Hoboken, N.J.: John Wiley & Sons. pp. 3-19 and 35-39.

Nelson, C., Furtado, E., Fox, A., & Zeanah, C. (2009). The deprived human brain. *American Scientist,* 97, 222-229. http://www.americanscientist.org/ issues/id.6380,y.2009,no.3,content. true,page.4,css.print/issue.aspx

NICHD Early Child Care Research Network (1996). Characteristics of infant child care: Factors contributing to positive caregiving. Early Childhood Research Quarterly, 11. pp. 296-306.

NICHD Early Child Care Research Network (2000). Characteristics and quality of child care for toddlers and preschoolers. Applied Developmental Science, 4(3). pp. 116-125.

Nodelman, P. and Reimer, M. (2003). The pleasures of children's literature. Boston: Allyn and Bacon. pp. 1-329.

Piaget, J. (1952[1936]). The origins of intelligence in children. International University Press.

Piaget, J. & Szeminska, A. (1941). The child's conception of number. Selected pages reprinted in Gruber, H.E.& Voneche, J.J. (1977). *The essential Piaget*. New Jersey: Jason Aronson Inc. pp. 298-311.

Prensky, M. (2000). Digital game-based learning. New York: McGraw-Hill.

Prensky, M. (2001a). Digital natives, digital immigrants. *On the Horizon* 9 (5). pp.1-6. http://www.scribd.com/doc/9799/Prensky-Digital-Natives-Digital-Immigrants-Part1. Archived at http://www.webcitation.org/5eBDYI5Uw.

Prensky, M. (2001b). Digital natives, digital immigrants, part 2: Do they really think differently? *On the Horizon* 9 (6). pp. 1-6. http://www.twitchspeed.com/site/Prensky%20-%20Digital%20Natives,%20Digital%20Immigrants%20-%20Part2.htm. Archived at http://www.webcitation.org/5eBDhJB2N.

Prensky, M. (2009). Innovate: Journal of Online Education. "H. Sapiens Digital: From Digital Immigrants and Digital Natives to Digital Wisdom". 5(3). http://www.innovateonline.info/index.php?view=article&id=705&action=login

Prensky, M. (2006). Don't bother me, mom: I'm learning. New York: Paragon.

Ratey, J. (2001). A user's guide to the brain. New York: Pantheon Books. pp. 1-378.

Ratey, J. and Hagerman, E. (2008). Spark: The revolutionary new science of exercise and the brain. New York: Little Brown and Company. pp. 1-268.

Repitti R., Taylor S., Seeman T. (2002). Risky families: Family social environments and the mental and physical health of offspring. *Psychological Bulletin,*128. pp. 330-366.

http://repettilab.psych.ucla.edu/repetti%20taylor%20seeman%202002.pdf

Restak, R. (2002). The secret life of the brain. New York: Pantheon Books.

Restak, R. (2003). The new brain: How the modern age is rewiring your mind. New York: Rodale Press.

Richardson, W. (2010). Blogs, wikis, podcasts, and other powerful web tools for classrooms. Thousand Oaks, CA: Corwin. pp. 1-160.

Richardson, W. and Mancabelli, R. (2011). Personal learning networks: Using the power of connections to transform education. Bloomington, IN: Solution Tree Press. pp. 1-142.

Rideout, V., Roberts, D., and Foehr, U. (2005). *Generation M: Media in the lives of 8-18 year-olds.* Executive summary. Menlo Park, CA: Henry J. Kaiser Family Foundation.

Rideout, V., Roberts, D., and Foehr, U. (2010). *Generation M2: Media in the lives of 8-18 year-olds.* Executive summary. Menlo Park, CA: Henry J. Kaiser Family Foundation.

Rideout, V., and Hamel, E. (2006). *The media family: Electronic media in the lives of infants, toddlers, preschoolers, and their parents.* Menlo Park, CA: Henry J. Kaiser Family Foundation.

Rose, D. and Dalton, B. (2009). Learning to read in the digital age. *Mind, Brain, and Education,* 3(2). Pp. 74-83.

Rose, D. and Gavel, J. (2012). Curricular opportunities in the digital age. Students at the center series, Boston: Jobs for the future. Retrieved online from www.studentsatthecenter.org/papers/curricular-opportunities-digital-age.

Rose, D. and Meyer, A. (2002). Teaching every student in the digital age: Universal design for learning. Alexandria, VA: Association for Supervision and Curriculum Development. pp. 1-174.

Rose, L. T. & Fischer, K. W. (2009). Dynamic systems theory. In R.A. Shweder (Ed.), *Chicago Companion to the Child.* Chicago: University of Chicago Press. pp. 1-6.

Sadler, W. (2009). *Langman's medical embryology, eleventh edition: North American edition.* Philadelphia, PA: Lippincott Williams & Wilkins (pp. 36-54, 293-300).

Sapolsky, R., Romero, L., & Munck, A. (2000). How do glucorticoids influence stress responses? Integrating permissive, suppressive, stimulatory and preparative actions. *Endocrine Reviews,* 21(1), pp. 55-89.

Sapolsky, R. (2004). Why zebras don't have ulcers: An updated guide to stress, stress related diseases, and coping (3rd ed.). New York: Owl Books.

Seligman, M. with Reivich, K., Jaycox, L. and Gillham, J. (1995). The optimistic child: A proven program to safeguard children against depression and build lifelong resilience. New York: Houghton Mifflin. pp. 1-305.

Schmidt, M., and Anderson, D. (2006). The impact of television on cognitive development and educational achievement. In N. Pecora, J. P. Murray, and E. A. Wartella, (Eds.). *Children and television: Fifty years of research.* Mahwah, NJ: Lawrence Erlbaum Associates.

Schwartz, T. (2010). Be excellent at anything: The four keys to transforming the way we work and live. NY: Free Press. pp. 1-275.

Shonkoff, J. and Phillips, D. (Eds.). (2000). From neurons to neighborhoods: The Science of early childhood development. National Research Council and Institute of Medicine. Washington, D.C.: National Academy Press. pp. 1-413.

Shonkoff, J., Boyce, W.T., & McEwen, B.S. (2009). Neuroscience, molecular biology, and the childhood roots of health disparities: Building a new framework for health promotion and disease prevention. *Journal of the American Medical Association,* 301, 2252-2259.

Shonkoff, J. (2000). Science, policy, and practice: Three cultures in search of a shared mission. *Child Development,* 71. pp. 181-187.

Siegler, R. (2003). Implications of cognitive science research for mathematics education. In J. Kilpatrick, W.B. Martin, & D.E. Schifter (Eds.), *A research companion to principles and standards for school mathematics*. Reston, VA: National Council of Teachers of Mathematics. pp. 219-233.

Silvey, A. (Ed.). (2002). The essential guide to children's books and their creators. NY: Houghton Mifflin. pp. 1-498.

Simpson, A. Rae. (2001). Raising teens: A synthesis of research and a foundation for action. Boston: Center for Health Communication, Harvard School of Public Health. pp. 1-68.

Singer, D. and Singer, J. (Eds.). (2001). *Handbook of children and the media*. Thousand Oaks, CA: Sage Publications.

Smith, S., Smith, S., Pieper, K., Yoo, K., Ferris, A., Downs, E and Bowden, B. (2006). Altruism on american television: Examining the amount of, and context surrounding, acts of helping and sharing. *Journal of Communication, 56*, pp. 707-727.

Society for Neuroscience. (2006). Brain facts: A primer on the brain and nervous system. *Sleep*. *Stress*. Canada. pp. 4-60.

Spitzer, M. (2000). The mind within a net. Cambridge, MA: MIT Press.

Steele, C. (1997). A threat in the air: How stereotypes shape intellectual identity and performance. *American Psychologist, 52*(6), pp. 613-629.

Stein, Z., Dawson, T. & Fischer, K. (2010). Redesigning testing: Operationalizing the new science of learning. In Khine &Saleh (Eds.). *The new science of learning: Computers, cognition and collaboration education*. Springer Press.

Sternberg, R. (1996). Successful intelligence: How practical and creative intelligence determine success in life. New York: Simon and Schuster.

Sternberg, R. (1997). Thinking Styles. Cambridge: University Press.

Sylvan, L. and Christodoulou, J. (2010). Understanding the role of neuroscience in brain-based products: A guide for educators and consumers. *Mind, Brain, and Education*, 4(1). pp. 1-7.

Sylwester, R. (2007). The adolescent brain reaching for autonomy. Thousand Oaks, CA: Corwin Press. pp.1-139.

Szucs, D. & Goswami, U., (2007). Educational neuroscience: Defining a new discipline for the study of mental representations. *Mind, Brain, and Education*, 1(3), pp. 114-127.

Szyf, M. (2009a). Early life, the epigenome and human health. Acta Paediatrica, 98(7). pp. 1082-1084.

Szyf, M. (2009b). The early life environment and the epigenome. Biochimica Biophysica Acta (BBA), 1790(9). pp. 878-885.

Thompson, R. and Nelson, C. (2001). Developmental science and the media. American Psychologist, 56(1). pp. 5-15.

Thompson, R. & Lagattuta, K. (2006). Feeling and understanding: Early emotional development. In K. McCartney & D. Phillips (Eds.), The Blackwell Handbook of Early Childhood Development. Oxford, UK: Blackwell. pp. 317-337.

Trelease, J. (2006). The read-aloud handbook. NY: Penguin Group. pp. 1-318.

Vygotsky, L. (1978). Mind and society: The development of higher psychological processes. Cambridge, MA: MIT Press.

Vygotsky, L. (1986). Thought and language. Cambridge, MA: MIT Press. pp. 190-208.

Waldfogel, J. (1999).The impact of the family and medical leave act. Journal of Policy Analysis and Management, 18(2). pp. 281-302.

Weinberger, D., Elvevag, B. & Giedd, J. (2005). The adolescent brain: A work in progress. The National Campaign to Prevent Teen Pregnancy. TEENPREGNANCY.org

Weiss, C.H. (1995). Nothing as practical as good theory: Exploring theory-based evaluation for comprehensive community initiatives for children and families. In J.P. Connell, A.C. Kubisch, L.B. Schorr, & C.H. Weiss (Eds.), New approaches to evaluating community initiatives: Concepts, methods and contexts (pp. 65-92). Washington , DC: The Aspen Institute. http://aspe.hhs.gov/pic/reports/aspe/5895.pdf#page=83
Weissbourd, R. (2009). The parents we mean to be: How well-intentioned adults undermine children's moral and emotional development. New York: Houghton Mifflin Harcourt Brace Publishing. pp. 1-206.

Weaver, I., Diorio, J., Seckl, J., Szyf, M., & Meaney, M. (2004) Early environmental regulation of hippocampal glucocorticoid receptor gene expression: Characterization of intracellular mediators and potential genomic target sites. Annals of the New York Academy of Sciences, 1024. pp. 182-212.

Wolf, M. (2007). Proust and the squid: The story and science of the reading brain. New York: HarperCollins Publishers. pp. 1-236.

Worden, J., Hinton, C. & Fischer, K. (2011). What does the brain have to do with learning? Phi Delta Kappan, 92(8). pp. 8-11.

Yoshikawa, H., & Hsueh, J. (2001). Child development and public policy: Toward a dynamic systems perspective. Child Development, 72, 1887-1903.

Zito, J., Safer, D., dosReis, S., Gardner, J., Boles, M., & Lynch, F. (2000).Trends in the prescribing of psychotropic medications to preschoolers. Journal of the American Medical Association, 283(8). pp. 1025-1030.

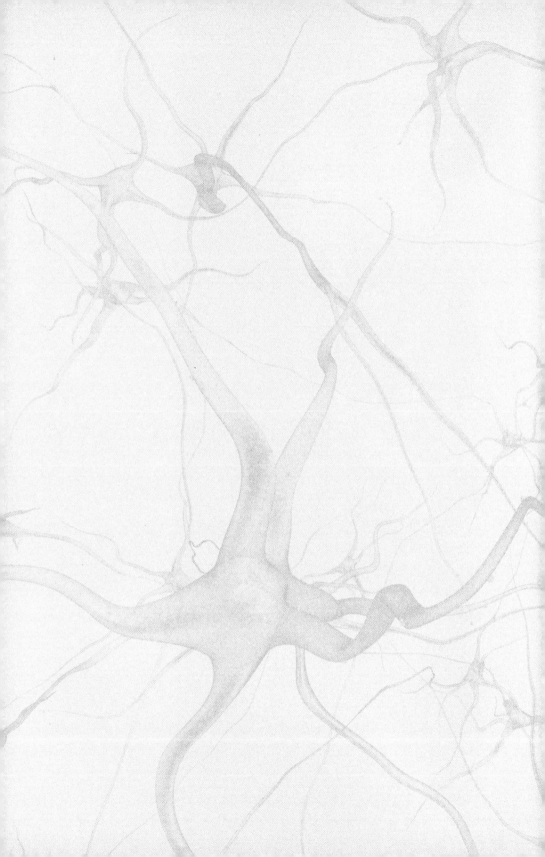